Alfred Gudeman

Outlines of the History of Classical Philology

Second Edition

Alfred Gudeman

Outlines of the History of Classical Philology
Second Edition

ISBN/EAN: 9783337179144

Printed in Europe, USA, Canada, Australia, Japan

Cover: Foto ©Thomas Meinert / pixelio.de

More available books at **www.hansebooks.com**

OUTLINES

OF THE

HISTORY OF CLASSICAL PHILOLOGY

BY

ALFRED GUDEMAN
UNIVERSITY OF PENNSYLVANIA

SECOND EDITION, REVISED AND ENLARGED

Genera degustamus, non bibliothecas excutimus. — QUINTILIAN

BOSTON, U.S.A.
GINN & COMPANY, PUBLISHERS
1894

COPYRIGHT, 1894
BY ALFRED GUDEMAN

ALL RIGHTS RESERVED

PREFATORY NOTE.

THE present edition, enlarged and revised throughout, has been in particular augmented by the addition of the lists of Latin Scholia and Grammatical Terms, as suggested by my reviewers.

The favorable reception accorded to this survey of the history of classical philology possibly justifies the hope that this new edition may facilitate the general introduction of so important and interesting a subject into the classical curriculum of the Universities of England and America.

A. G.

PHILADELPHIA, Oct. 12, 1894.

CONTENTS.

A. General Introduction.

		PAGE
I. Φιλόλογος, γραμματικός, κριτικός		1
II. PHILOLOGY IN MODERN TIMES		5
III. METHODS OF TREATMENT		5

B. History of Classical Philology.

I. GREEK PERIOD.
   1. Pre-Alexandrian 6
   2. Alexandrian 9
   3. The Stoics and the School of Pergamum 21

II. GRAECO-ROMAN PERIOD.
   1. Post-Alexandrian 23
      List of Greek Scholia 27
      Critical Signs 28
      Grammatical Terms (Greek and Latin) 30
   2. Roman Period 33
      List of Latin Scholia 40

III. MIDDLE AGES.
   1. Byzantian Period 41
   2. W. Europe 45
      List of Oldest MSS. 46

IV. REVIVAL OF LEARNING IN ITALY.
   (A) Greek Immigrants 47
   (B) Italian Humanists 48
      List of Editiones Principes 51

V. FRANCE 53

VI. THE NETHERLANDS.

1. First Period 56
2. Second Period 56
3. Third Period 58
4. Fourth Period 60

VII. ENGLAND 61

VIII. GERMANY.

(A) *Ante-Wolfian Period* 63
(B) *The New School* 66
    1. Grammatico-critical School 67
    2. Historico-antiquarian School 70

C. Index of Names 75

OUTLINES OF THE HISTORY OF CLASSICAL PHILOLOGY.

La philologie c'est la géologie du monde intellectuel.
                                            BENOIST.

A. General Introduction.

I. *a.* Φιλόλογος — its original meaning and semasiological development.

First met with in *Plato* (e.g. Theaet., p. 146 *a* ; Laches, p. 188 ; Rep., p. 582 ; Leges, p. 641 *e*). Opp. to μισόλογος, βραχύλογος. Equivalent to πολύλογος, φιλόσοφος. φιλολογία = παιδεία (μουσική). Cf. *Plato*, Phaed. 61 *a* ;- Isoc. de Antid. 296 : εὐτραπελίαν καὶ φιλολογίαν οὐ μικρὸν ἡγοῦνται συμβαλέσθαι μέρος, πρὸς τὴν τῶν λόγων παιδείαν, etc.

Alexandrian Period: Equivalent to φιλομαθής, πολυίστωρ (cf. *Plut.* Alex., c. 8). In this sense first applied to *Eratosthenes*, and among the Romans to *Ateius Capito*. Cf. *Sueton.* de gram., p. 108 R. " Philologi appellationem assumpsisse videtur quia, sicut Eratosthenes qui primus hoc cognomen sibi vindicavit, multiplici variaque doctrina censebatur."

Roman Period: φιλολογεῖν = learned conversation. Cf. *Cic.* ad fam. XVI 21 ; *Plut.* Cato Min. 6 ; *Ps. Plut.* Vit. X Orat., p. 844 D. φιλόλογοι opp. to πολιτικοί — *Plut.* Lyc. 42. Opp. to φιλόσοφος — Vita Plotini, p. 116 : φιλόλογος˙μὲν ὁ Λογγῖνος, φιλόσοφος δὲ μηδαμῶς. Opp. to ἀπαίδευτος — *Stob.* Floril. 428, 53. Philologus = vir studiosus, doctus — *Cic.* ad Att. XIII 12, 3; *Plut.* de aud. poet. 30 *d.* More closely allied to philologist in the modern sense in *Seneca*, Ep. 108, 29, quoted below.

b. Γραμματικός (γραμματική, sc. τέχνη) — its original meaning and semasiological development.

Conversant with γράμματα (*Plato*, Phil. 17 ; Crat., p. 341 ; *Arist. Pol.* VIII 3 ; Categ. 9). γραμματιστής = a teacher of γράμματα (*Plato*, Prot. 312 ; Legg. VII 812). *Alexandrian Period: Clem. Alex.* Στρωμ. I, p. 309 : Ἀπολλόδωρος (Ἀντόδωρος?) ὁ Κυμαῖος (Cf. Susemihl *Alex. Lit.* II, p. 664) πρῶτος τοῦ κριτικοῦ εἰσηγήσατο τοὔνομα καὶ γραμματικὸς προσηγορεύθη. Ἔνιοι δὲ Ἐρατοσθένη τὸν Κυρηναῖον φασὶν ἐπειδὴ ἐξέδωκεν οὗτος βιβλία δύο γραμματικὰ ἐπιγράψας. ὠνομάσθη δὲ γραμματικός, ὡς νῦν (3d cent.) ὀνομάζομεν, πρῶτος Πραξιφάνης (c. 300 B.C.). Γραμματική acc. to *Dionysius Thrax:* Ἐμπειρία ὡς ἐστὶ τὸ πλεῖστον τῶν παρὰ ποιηταῖς τε καὶ συγγραφεῦσι λεγομένων. Six subdivisions :

1. Ἀνάγνωσις ἐντριβὴς κατὰ προσῳδίαν ⎫
2. Ἐξήγησις κατὰ ποιητικοὺς τρόπους   ⎬ = τέχνη
3. Γλωσσῶν καὶ ἱστοριῶν πρόχειρος ἀπόδοσις ⎪ μικρά,
4. Ἐτυμολογίας εὕρεσις   ⎪ ἀτελεστέρα.
5. Ἀναλογίας ἐκλογισμός   ⎭
6. Κρίσις ποιημάτων — ὃ δὴ κάλλιστόν ἐστι πάντων ἐν τῇ τέχνῃ } = τ. μακρά, ἐντελής.

Sext. Emp. adv. Gramm. I 4 (according to Apollonios Dyscolos?) Γραμματική : 1. τεχνικόν ; 2. ἱστορικόν ; 3. ἰδιαίτερον. a. ἐξηγητικόν ; b. κριτικόν ; c. διορθωτικόν. *Roman Period : Sueton.* de gramm., p. 103 Rf. : "Appellatio grammaticorum Graeca consuetudine invaluit sed initio *litterati* vocabantur. Cornelius quoque Nepos libello quo distinguit litteratum ab erudito, litteratos vulgo quidem appellari ait eos qui diligenter aliquid et acute scienterque possint aut dicere aut scribere, ceterum proprie sic appellandos poetarum interpretes qui a Graecis grammatici nominentur." *Cic.* de orat. I 42,

187 : grammatica = poetarum pertractio, historiarum cognitio, verborum interpretatio, pronuntiandi quidem sonus ; cp. also Orat. I 22 ; de div. I 11 ; *Quint.* I 2, 14 : si de loquendi ratione disserat (sc. grammaticus), si quaestiones explicet, historias exponat, poemata enarret. II 1, 4 grammatice quam in Latinum transferentes *litteraturam* vocaverunt.

c. Κριτικός.

Among the Greeks: First found in *Ps. Plat.* Axioch. 366 *E:* ὁπόταν δὲ εἰς τὴν ἑπταετίαν ἀφίκηται πολλοὺς πόνους διαντλῆσαν, παιδαγωγοὶ καὶ γραμματισταὶ καὶ παιδοτριβαὶ τυραννοῦντες. αὐξομένου δὲ κριτικοί, γεωμέτραι, τακτικοί, πολὺ πλῆθος δεσποτῶν. Κριτικός as a synonym of γραμματικός. Γραμματική sometimes made subordinate to κριτική. Cf. *Schol. ad Dionys. Thr.*, p. 673, 19 : ἐπιγέγραπται γὰρ τὸ παρὸν σύγγραμμα κατὰ μέν τινας περὶ γραμματικῆς, κατὰ δὲ ἑτέρους περὶ κριτικῆς τέχνης. κριτικὴ δὲ λέγεται ἡ τέχνη ἐκ τοῦ καλλίστου μέρους. *Bekker, Anecd. Gr.*, p. 1140 : τὸ πρότερον κριτικὴ ἐλέγετο (sc. ἡ γραμματικὴ) καὶ οἱ ταύτην μετίοντες κριτικοί. *Dio Chrys.* 53 : οὐ μόνον Ἀρίσταρχος καὶ Κράτης καὶ ἕτεροι πλείους τῶν ὕστερον γραμματικῶν κληθέντων, πρότερον δὲ κριτικῶν. *Sext. Emp.* adv. Gramm., § 248 : Ταυρίσκος γοῦν ὁ Κράτητος ἀκουστὴς ὥσπερ οἱ ἄλλοι κριτικοί, ὑποτάσσων τῇ κριτικῇ τὴν γραμματικήν, etc.

Among the Romans: Cic. ad fam. IX 10, 1 (quoted by *Suet.*, p. 111) : profert alter, opinor, duobus versiculis expensum Niciae ; alter Aristarchus hos ὀβελίζει. Ego tamquam *criticus* antiquus iudicaturus sum, utrum sint τοῦ ποιητοῦ an παρεμβεβλημένοι. *Hor.* Ep. II 1, 51 : ut *critici* dicunt. Apparently not found elsewhere in Latin (for in Quint. II 1, 4 the reading is doubtful), *grammaticus* being the word commonly used. For the distinction between the various termini, see the locus classicus

in *Senec.* Ep. 108, 29 : Cum Ciceronis librum de republica prendit hinc *philologus* aliquis, hinc *grammaticus*, hinc *philosophiae* deditus alius alio curam suam mittit. *Philosophus* admiratur contra iustitiam dici tam multa potuisse. Cum ad hanc eandem lectionem *philologus* accessit, hoc subnotat : duos Romanos reges esse, quorum alter patrem non habet, alter patrem : nam de Servii matre dubitatur. Anci pater nullus, Numae nepos dicitur. Praeterea notat eum, quem nos dictatorem dicimus et in historiis ita nominari legimus, apud antiquos magistrum populi vocatum. Hodieque id exstat in auguralibus libris et testimonium est quod qui ab illo nominetur, magister equitum est. Aeque notat Romulum perisse solis defectione, provocationem ad populum etiam a regibus fuisse ; id ita in pontificalibus libris et alii putant et Fenestella. Eosdem libros cum *grammaticus* explicuit primum verba expressa, reapse dici a Cicerone id est re ipsa, in commentarium refert nec minus sepse id est se ipse, deinde transit ad ea quae consuetudo saeculi mutavit tamquam ait Cicero.. 'ab ipsa calce.. revocati' hanc quam nunc in circo cretam vocamus, calcem antiqui dicebant. Deinde Ennianos colligit versus et in primis illos de Africano scriptos ... Felicem deinde se putat quod invenerit unde visum sit Vergilio dicere, 'quem super ingens porta tonat caeli' — Ennium, hoc ait, Homero subripuisse, Ennio Vergilium, esse enim apud Ciceronem in his ipsis de republica libris hoc epigramma Enni.

Cf. *I. Classen*, De grammaticae Graecae primordiis ; Bonn, 1829. *Lobeck*, Phrynichus, pp. 392 ff. *K. Lehrs*, De vocabulis φιλόλογος, γραμματικός, κριτικός (Appendix to Herodiani Scripta Tria, Berlin, 1857). *Gräfenhan*, Gesch. der class. Philologie, I, 336 ff. III, 4 ff. *Steinthal*, Gesch. d. Sprachwissenschaft bei den Griech. u. Röm. II², 14 ff. *Susemihl*, Gesch. der Alexand. Literat. I, 327 (see below).

II. PHILOLOGY IN MODERN TIMES:

Its various definitions, subdivisions and its scope.

In a *narrower* sense—Grammar, Lexicology, Textual Criticism, Hermeneutics, aesthetic or literary criticism ('Higher Criticism').

In a *wider* sense, it includes the study of ancient life in all its various, political, social and intellectual phases, as handed down to us in the literary, epigraphic and monumental documents of Greece and Rome.

<small>*Fr. Ast*, Grundriss der Philol. 1808; *G. Bernhardy*, Grundlinien z. Encycl. der Philol. 1832; *Fr. Haase*, Ersch. u. Gruber Encycl. III Sect. 23 pp. 374–422; *Fr. Ritschl*, Opusc. V 1 ff.; *H. Reichardt*, Die Gliederung der Philologie 1846; *C. Hirzel*, Grundzüge zu einer Gesch. der Philol. 1872², pp. 41; *Aug. Boeckh*, Encyclop. und Methodol. 1886.</small>

III. METHODS OF TREATMENT.
1. The SYNCHRONISTIC or ANNALISTIC METHOD.
    a. History of a *single period*. E.g. the Alexandrian, the Renaissance.
    b. Philological history of a *single author*. E.g. Homeric criticism; Aristotle, history of his works (Shute).
    c. History of an *individual scholar* and his influence (Biography and Bibliography). E.g. *Monk*, Life of Bentley; *O. Ribbeck*, Ritschl, 'Ein Beitrag zur Gesch. der class. Philologie'; *D. Ruhnken*, Elogium Hemsterhusii; *Wyttenbach*, Vita Ruhnkenii; *M. Pattison*, Casaubon.
2. The EIDOGRAPHIC METHOD.
    a. e.g. The science of Greek Grammar (Bernhardy, Steinthal).
    b. e.g. The history of Hermeneutics and Textual Criticism (Blass), Epigraphy (Larfeld, Hübner, Mommsen).

3. The ETHNOGRAPHIC or GEOGRAPHIC METHOD.
   a. *History of a particular school*, e.g. at Alexandria or in Pergamum (Parthey, Wegener).
   b. *Philological history of a single nation*, e.g. the Germans (Bursian), the Dutch (L. Müller).

B. History of Classical Philology.

General bibliography: *I. A. Fabricius*, Bibliotheca Graeca, ed. Harles; 12 vols., 1809. *Id.*, Bibliotheca Latina, ed. Ernesti; 2 vols., 1774. *E. Hübner*, Bibliographie der classischen Alterthumswissenschaft; Berlin, 1889^2. *Urlichs*, in I. Müller's Handbuch, I 1^2, pp. 1–145.

I. THE GREEK PERIOD (5 cent.–146 B.C.).

Bibliography: *Gräfenhan*, Gesch. der class. Philologie, 4 vols.; Bonn, 1843–50. *Lersch*, Sprachphilosophie der Alten, 1841. *Steinthal*, Geschichte der Sprachwissenschaft bei den Griechen u. Römern, 2 vols.; Berlin, 1891^2. *E. Egger*, Essai sur l'Histoire de la Critique chez les Grecs; Paris, 1886^2, pp. 570.

1. THE PRE-ALEXANDRIAN PERIOD, 5. cent.–322 († Aristotle).
   a. *The alleged recension of Homer by Peisistratus.*
      Cf. *Wilamowitz*, Homer. Untersuch., p. 235 ff. *Flach*, Peisistratus u. seine literarische Thätigkeit; Tübingen, 1885. Also *Ritschl*, Opusc. I, 31–60. 123 ff. 160–67. 196 ff.
   b. *The Sophists.*
      Cf. *W. O. Friedel*, De sophistarum studiis Homericis, Diss. Hallens. I, 1873, pp. 127 ff. *Gräfenhan*, I, 124–41. *L. Spengel*, Συναγωγὴ τεχνῶν, 1828. *Westermann*, Griech. Beredsamkeit, 1832. *Blass*, Griech. Beredsamkeit, Vol. I. *Cope*, Aristotle's Rhetoric, Vol. I, Introduction.
      α. *Gorgias* of Leontini (arrived at Athens 427 B.C.). Περὶ ὀνομάτων συνθέσεως — ἰσόκωλα πάρισα ὁμοιοτέλευτα. Oral instruction. A treatise on rhetoric falsely attributed to him by Dionysius, Diogenes, Laertius and Quintilian. Cf. the literature cited above.

β. *Protagoras* of Abdera († 411 B.C.).
Περὶ ὀρθοεπείας— P. the first to distinguish grammatical moods and genders. Cp. *Aristoph.* Clouds, vv. 659 ff.

Cf. *Classen*, l. c., p. 28; *Lersch*, l. c., pp. 18 ff.; *Spengel*, pp. 52 ff., and the citations given above.

γ. *Prodicus* of Ceos (older contemporary of Socrates). Founder of synonymics.

Cf. *Spengel*, l. c., pp. 46 ff.; *Lersch*, pp. 15 ff.; *Welcker*, Rh. Mus. I, 1–39, 563–643 (= Kl. *Schr.* II, 393–541).

c. *Literary Criticism in Attic Comedy.*

Cp. *Egger*, l. c., pp. 37–89.

d. *Plato* (427–347) as a philologist.
  (1) Grammar (ὄνομα, ῥῆμα).
  (2) Etymology (esp. in the *Cratylus*).
  (3) Exegesis (Poem of Simonides in the *Protagoras*).
  (4) Aesthetic or Literary Criticism (esp. in the *Republic*).

Cf. *Steinthal* I^2, 41–152 (on the Cratylus).

e. *The official copy of the three dramatists.*

Cf. O. *Korn*, De publico Aesch., Soph., Eurip., fabularum exemplari Lycurgo auctore confecto, Bonn, 1863; *Wilamowitz*, Hermes, XIV, 151; Eurip. Heracl. I, 130.

f. ARISTOTLE of Stagira, 384–322.
  Dio Chrysost. LIII, p. 353 (294 R.): Ἀριστοτέλης, ἀφ' οὗ φασι τὴν κριτικήν τε καὶ γραμματικὴν ἀρχὴν λαβεῖν.
  (1) Edition of *Homer* (ἡ ἀπὸ τοῦ νάρθηκος; cf. Plut. Alex. 8: Strabo, XIII 594; Schol. Iliad. XXI 252; Schol. Theocr. I 34—Προβλήματα (?)).
  (2) Grammar, style, *rhetoric* (Poet. c. 24 ff.: Rhet., bk. III).
  (3) *Aesthetic* criticism (Poetics, Περὶ ποιητῶν).
  (4) Διδασκαλίαι, C. I. G. I, 349 sqq.; C. I. A. II, 971–77.

Cf. *Ranke*, Vita Aristophanis (in Thiersch, Plutus, 1830), pp. 83 ff.; *Richter*, Arist. Wasps, Introd.; *U. Köhler*, Mittheil. d. Athen. Instit. III (1878), 112 f., 229 ff.

(5) Peplos — Cf. *A. Wendling*, De peplo A., Strassb. Diss. 1891.

g. The Peripatetic School.

α. *Heracleides Ponticus*, pupil of Plato and Aristotle.

Cf. *Gräfenhan*, II, 63; *Unger*, Rh. Mus. XXXVIII, 481 ff.; *L. Cohn*, Comment. Reiffersch., Breslau, 1884.

β. *Theophrastus* of Eresos, 372–287/6.
(1) Περὶ κωμῳδίας (Athen. 261 *d*).
(2) Περὶ λέξεως (Dionys. Hal. de Lys. c. 14).

Cf. *H. Usener*, De Dionysii Hal. imitatione reliquiae, Bonn, 1889. *Rabe*, De Th. libris Περὶ λέξεως, Bonn, 1890.

(3) Περὶ μέτρων, περὶ σολοικισμῶν, probably parts of (2). Cf. the catalogue of his writings given by Diog. Laert. (from Hermippos) V 42–50.

γ. *Aristoxenus ὁ μουσικός, of Tarentum.*

Περὶ τραγῳδοποιῶν (esp. on Soph.), περὶ τραγικῆς ὀρχήσεως, Σύμμικτα ὑπομνήματα, περὶ μουσικῆς, περὶ μελοποιίας — Βίοι (philosophers and tragedians). Cf. *W. L. Mahne*, Diatribe de A., 1793, pp. 220.

δ. *Dicaearchus*, 347–287.

Ὑποθέσεις τῶν Εὐριπίδου καὶ Σοφοκλέους μύθων (hypothesis to Eur. Medea still extant).

Περὶ μουσικῶν ἀγώνων (Schol. Arist. Ran. 1335; Vesp. 1290).

Cf. *F. Osann*, Beitr. zur griech. u. röm. Litteraturgesch. II, 1839, pp. 1 ff.; *Pauly*, R. E. II, 996 ff.; *M. Fuhr*, Dicaearchi quae supersunt etc., 1841; *Fabricius*, Bibl. Gr. III, 486–491.

h. Praxiphanes of Rhodes or Mytilene, floruit c. 300.

'Πρῶτος γραμματικός'; vid. Clem. Alex. cited above.

Teacher of Aratus and Callimachus.

Works: Περὶ ποιητῶν, περὶ ἱστορίας, περὶ ποιημάτων.

Cf. L. *Preller*, De Praxiphane (Ausgewählte Aufsätze, Berlin, 1864); *Susemihl*, I, 144 ff.; *Wilamowitz*, Hermes, XII, 326 ff.; Eur. Heracl. I, 16 Anm. 25; *R. Hirzel*, Hermes, XIII, 46 ff.; *R. Schöll*, ibid. pp. 446 f.

i. Antigonos of Carystos, born c. 295.
(1) Lives of *contemporary philosophers*.
(2) Lives of *Greek sculptors and painters*.

Cf. *Wilamowitz*, Antigonos von Carystos (Philol. Unters. IV, 356); *Susemihl*, I, 468–75. 519–23. II, 675.

2. THE ALEXANDRIAN PERIOD, 322 (or 305)–143 (†Aristarchus).

Chief work : *F. Susemihl*, Gesch. d. griech. Literat. in der Alexand. Zeit, 2 vols., 1892, pp. 907. 771.

General characteristics of the period. The great Library and Museum. Cf. *Couat*, pp. 1–50; *Susemihl*, I, 335 ff.; *Parthey*, Das Alexandrin. Museum, Berlin, 1838; *Ritschl*, Opusc. I, 1–70. 123–72. 197–237; *Bernhardy*, Gesch. d. griech. Literat. I⁴, 509–43 II, 699 ff.; *Wilamowitz*, Eur. Heracl., I, 121 ff.; *Renan, E.*, Mélanges d'histoire dans l'antiquité, Paris, 1878 (Les grammairiens grecs pp. 389–410. 427–440).

a. Philetas of Cos, 339–289/5.

Ἄτακτα (Ἄτακτοι γλῶσσαι, Γλῶσσαι). The first attempt at a Homeric lexicon. Cf. Aristarchus, Πρὸς Φιλητᾶν.

On *Philetas* as a poet, vide *Couat*, La Poésie Alexandrine, Paris, 1882, pp. 68 ff.; *Susemihl*, I, 174 ff.

b. Zenodotus of Ephesus, c. 325–c. 260.
Pupil of Philetas. *First* librarian of Alexandria.
(1) Collection of the works of the *epic* and *lyric* poets. Cf. Schol. Plautinum ; Ritschl, Opusc. l. c.
(2) Γλῶσσαι Ὁμηρικαί (Schol. Od. 3, 444; Schol. Apoll. Rhod. II 1005).
(3) Διόρθωσις (or ἔκδωσις) Ὁμήρου, the first scientific edition of the Iliad and the Odyssey. Published shortly before 274 B.C.

On his critical method, cf. *F. A. Wolf,* Proleg. c. 43; *Sengebusch,* Diss. Hom. I, 21 ff.; *Düntzer,* De Zenodoti studiis Homericis, Göttingen, 1848; *Römer,* Ueber die Homerrecension des Zenodot (Münchner Acad. I, Cl. XVII, 639-722 (1885); *Susemihl,* I, 327-35; *Pusch,* Quaest. Zenod. (Diss. Hall. XI, 119-216).

c. *Alexander Aetolus,* floruit c. 285 B.C.

Collection of the *Greek tragic poets* in the Alexand. Library.

Cf. *Ritschl,* l. c., pp. 2-4. 199 f. On his poetry : *Meineke,* Anal. Alex. pp. 215 ff.; *Susemihl,* I, 187-90; *Couat,* pp. 105 ff.

d. *Lycophron of Chalcis,* c. 285 B.C.

(1) Collection of the *comic poets* in the Alexand. Library.

Cf. *Ritschl,* l. c.

(2) Περὶ κωμῳδίας in at least 9 books. The oldest work of its kind.

Cf. *K. Strecker,* De Lycophrone Euphronio Eratosthene comicorum interpretibus, Greifswald, 1884 (with collection of fragments); *Susemihl,* I, 274. 426.

e. CALLIMACHUS *of Cyrene,* c. 310-c. 240.

Second librarian of Alexandria. Μέγα βιβλίον, μέγα κακόν.

Chief work: Πίνακες τῶν ἐν πάσῃ παιδείᾳ διαλαμψάντων καὶ ὧν συνέγραψαν, 120 books. On the classification and contents of this catalogue :

Cf. *O. Schneider,* Callimachea, II, 297-322; *Wachsmuth,* Philol. XVI, 653 ff.; *Gräfenhan,* II, 182 ff.; *Susemihl,* I, 337 f. On the *Homeric* studies of C., cf. *F. von Ian,* De C. Homeri interprete, Strassb. Diss. 1893, pp. 110.—On C. as a poet, cf. *Couat,* pp. 111-284; *Susemihl,* I, 347-73.

f. ERATOSTHENES *of Cyrene,* c. 276-196.

Ὁ φιλόλογος, the first to assume that name. Cf. *Sueton.* p. 108 R. *Third* librarian of Alexandria. One of the most versatile and learned scholars of all time (ὁ πένταθλος, Βῆτα, cf. *Suidas* s. v. Ἐρατοσθένης.)

(1) Γεωγραφικά, 3 books. The first scientific treatment of the subject.

Cf. *Berger*, Gesch. der wissenschaftl. Erdkunde bei den Griech. III, 57-112, Lpz. 1891.

(2) Περὶ χρονογραφιῶν.
Cf. *Diels*, Rh. Mus. XXXI, 1 ff.; *Niese*, Hermes, XXIII, 92 ff.

(3) Ὀλυμπιονῖκαι.
Cf. *Bernhardy*, Eratosthenica, pp. 247 ff.

(4) Περὶ τῆς ἀρχαίας κωμῳδίας, in at least 12 books. "A philological masterpiece."
Cf. *Strecker*, l. c.; *Wilamowitz*, Hermes, XXI, 597 f. XXIV, 44; *Bernhardy*, l. c., pp. 203-37, and *Susemihl*, I, 409-28.

g. ARISTOPHANES *of Byzantium*, c. 257–c. 180.
Librarian, successor of Eratosthenes or Apollonius Rhodius. The greatest philologist of antiquity.

(1) *Invention* (?) *of accents, punctuation* (acc. to Arcadius, p. 186 ff.).
Cf. *Nauck*, pp. 12 ff.; *Wilamowitz*, l. c., pp. 127 f.; *Susemihl*, I, 432. 901; *Usener* ap. eundem, II, 672.

(2) Κριτικὰ σημεῖα. On the symbols themselves see below.
Cf. *Nauck*, pp. 15-18.

(3) *Editions* with critical signs to —
  α. *Homer* (Διόρθωσις Ὁμήρου). Cf. *Wolf*, Proleg. c. 44; *Nauck*, l. c., pp. 25-58. Close of the Odyssey, XXIII, 296. On his method of criticism, see *Wilamowitz* below.
  β. *Hesiod*, Theogony (cf. Schol. Theog. 68).
  γ. *Alcaeus, Anacreon, Pindar* and perhaps *Simonides* (Dionys. de comp. verb. 26).
  δ. *Euripides* (Schol. Or. 714. 1287; Hipp. 172).
Cf. *Nauck*, p. 62 f.
  ε. *Aristophanes* (Schol. Av. 1342; Thesm. 162. 917; Ran. 152 f.; Nub. 958).
Cf. *Nauck*, pp. 18. 63-66.
  ζ. *Menander* (?). Cf. his saying: "ὦ Μένανδρε καὶ βίε, πότερος ἄρ' ὑμῶν πότερον ἀπεμιμήσατο;"

(4) Ὑποθέσεις to Soph. Eur. Arist. and perhaps Aesch. (probably prefixed to his editions). Contents : Argument of the play, its sources, didascalia, aesthetic judgment. The following extant fragments of ὑποθέσεις are probably ultimately based upon those of Aristophanes :

Aeschylus: Persae, Sept. adv. Theb., *Agam.*, Eumen., Prom.

Sophocles: Oed. Col., Philoct., Ant. Oed. Rex (metrical) [Aiax].

Euripides: Hecuba, *Orest.*, *Phoen.*, Medea, *Hyppol.*, *Alcest.*, *Androm.*, Troad. [*Rhesos*], Ion, Iphig. Taur., Bacch., Heracleid., Helena, Hercul. Fur., Cyclops (none extant to Suppl., Iph. Aul., Electra).

Aristophanes: Acharn. I, II (metrical) ; Equit. I, II, III (met.) ; Nub. I, II, III, IV (met.), V, VI, VII ⟨VIII, IX, X⟩ ; Vesp. I, II (met.); Pax, I, II, III, IV (met.); Aves, I, II, III, IV (met.): Lysist. I, II (met.); Ranae, I, II (met.), ⟨III, IV⟩ ; Eccl. I, II (met.); Plut. I, II, III, IV, [V], VI (met.).

Cf. *F. W. Schneidewin*, De hypothesibus tragoed. Graec. Aristoph. Byz. vindicandis (Abh. der Gött. Gesell. der Wiss., Vol. IV, 1853–55); *Nauck*, l. c., pp. 255 ff.; *Trendelenburg*, Grammat. Graec. de arte trag. iudiciorum reliquiae, Bonn, 1867.

(5) Παράλληλοι Μενάνδρου τε καὶ ἀφ' ὧν ἔκλεψεν.

(6) Περὶ προσώπων (perhaps the ultimate source of Pollux, IV 133–54).

Cf. *Nauck*, pp. 275 ff. ; *Rohde*, De I. P. . . . fontibus, Lpz. 1870.

(7) Παροιμίαι (μετρικαὶ and ἄμετροι) in 6 books.

Cf. *Nauck*, pp. 235–42 ; *Leutsch*, Philol. III, 566.

(8) Περὶ ἀναλογίας.

Nauck, pp. 264 ff.

(9) Περὶ τῆς ἀχνυμένης σκυτάλης, a treatise on a passage in Archilochus (fragm. 89, 2).

Nauck, pp. 273 ff.

(10) Λέξεις — Περὶ τῶν ὑποπτευομένων μὴ εἰρῆσθαι τοῖς παλαιοῖς, περὶ ὀνομασίας ἡλικιῶν, περὶ συγγενικῶν ὀνομάτων — Ἀττικαὶ λέξεις, Λακωνικαὶ γλῶσσαι. The first scientific work on lexicography. About 100 fragments preserved.

Cf. *Nauck*, l. c., pp. 69-190; Rh. Mus. VI, 322-51; *Fresenius*, De λέξεων Aristophanearum et Suetoniarum excerptis Byzantinis, Wiesbaden, 1875; *L. Cohn*, Jahrb. f. Philol. Suppl. XII, 283-374.

(11) Πρὸς πίνακας Καλλιμάχου. Of this supplement to the great catalogue of Callimachus, the extant distribution of the Platonic Dialogues into trilogies (*Diog. Laert.* III 61 f.) formed probably a part.

(12) Κανόνες or lists of 'best authors.' Cf. *Quint.* X 1, 54 : "Apollonius in ordinem a grammaticis datum non venit quia Aristarchus atque Aristophanes neminem sui temporis in ordinem redegerunt"; vid. also X 1, 59 and I 4, 3.

For extant ancient lists cf. *Usener*, Dionysii Halic. librorum de imitatione reliquiae, Bonn, 1889, pp. 130 ff. On the probable character, contents and origin of these canones, cf. *Ranke*, Vita Aristoph., pp. 104 ff.; *Steffen*, De canone qui dicitur Aristophanis et Aristarchi, Lpz. 1876; *Brzoska*, De canone decem oratorum, Breslau, 1883; *P. Hartmann*, De canone decem oratorum, Göttingen, 1891, and *Susemihl*, I, 445. 484 II, 674 f. 694-97.

On *Aristophanes of Byzantium* in general cf. *A. Nauck*, Aristophanis Byzantii Fragmenta, Halle, 1848, pp. 338; *Susemihl*, I, 428-48; *Wilamowitz*, Eur. Heracles, I, 137-53.

h. ARISTARCHUS *of Samothrace*, 217/5-145/3.

Ὁμηρικός, ὁ κριτικός, πάνυ ἄριστος γραμματικός (Schol. Hom. B. 316) ὁ ἀνήρ (Herodianus in Schol. B. 153) μάντις (Athen. XIV 634). Hor. A. P. 450 fiet Aristarchus Cic. ad Att. I 14, 3 meis orationibus, quarum tu Aristarchus es. ad fam. IX 10, 1. 800 ὑπομνήματα. Difference betw. ὑπομνήματα and συγγράμ-

μάτα. The latter more highly esteemed than the former. Cf. *Didymus* (Schol. B 111): εἰ γὰρ τὰ συγγράμματα τῶν ὑπομνημάτων προτάττομεν.

(1) *Edition of Homer*. Two editions. Cf. *Lehrs*, p. 23; *Ludwig*, I, 17 ff. Cp. Schol. K 397: Ammonius, the successor of Aristarchus, the author of a treatise "Περὶ τοῦ μὴ γεγονέναι πλείονας (sc. τῶν δύο) ἐκδόσεις τῆς Ἀρισταρχείου διορθώσεως."

(2) Συγγράμματα — Περὶ Ἰλιάδος καὶ Ὀδυσσείας (Schol. I 349), Πρὸς Φιλητᾶν (Schol. A 524, B 111), Πρὸς Κωμανόν (Schol. A 97, B 798, Ω 110), Πρὸς τὸ Ξένωνος παράδοξον (Schol M 435 and *Susemihl*, II, 149 f.), Περὶ τοῦ ναυσταθμοῦ with a map or διάγραμμα (K 53, M 258, O 449, Λ 166, 807).

On his critical method cf. *Wolf*, Proleg., pp. 226 ff.; *Lehrs*, De Aristarchi studiis Homericis, Königsberg, 1882³ (1833¹); *Sengebusch*, Diss. Hom. I, 24 ff.; *Ludwig*, Aristarch's Homerische Textkritik nach den Fragmenten des Didymus, 2 vols., Lpz. 1885; *Wilamowitz*, Homer. Unters., pp. 383 ff.; Eurip. Heracles, I, 154; *Susemihl*, I, 451-63; *Jebb*, Homer, Boston, 1888, pp. 92 ff.

(3) Ὑπομνήματα 'commentaries' and ἐκδόσεις 'editions' with 'critical signs' to —

a. *Hesiod.*

Cf. *Flach*, Jahrb. f. Phil. 109 (1874), pp. 815 ff.; 115 (1877), pp. 433 ff.; *Waeschke*, De Aristarchi studiis Hesiodiis (Acta Sem. Lips. 1874); *Schömann*, Opusc. II, 510 ff. III, 47 ff.

β. Commentary to *Archilochus* (*Clem. Strom.* I 326 D).

γ. Edition of *Alcaeus* (*Hephaest.*, p. 136) and perhaps of *Anacreon*, certainly a commentary on this poet (*Athen.* XV 671 f., ἐξηγούμενος).

δ. *Pindar* (edition and commentary).

Feine, De Aristarcho Pindari interprete (Diss. Ienen. II, 253-327); *Horn*, De Aristarchi studiis Pindaricis, Greifswald, 1883; *Susemihl*, I, 460 ff.; *Lehrs*, Pindarscholien, Lpz. 1873.

ε. Commentary to *Aeschylus*, at all events to the Λυκοῦργος (Schol. *Theocr.* X 18). To *Ion*, at least to the Ὀμφάλη (*Athen.* XIV 634 c).

ζ. Commentaries to *Sophocles*.

Cf. *M. Schmidt*, Didymi fragmenta, Lpz. 1854, p. 262.

η. Commentary to *Aristophanes*.

O. Gerhard. De Aristarcho Aristophanis interprete, Bonn, 1850; *Schneider*, De Aristophanis schol. font., pp. 86 f.

(4) A.'s contributions to *grammar*. The first to distinguish *eight parts of speech*. Cf. *Quint.* I 4, 20; *Schömann*, Redetheile, p. 12; *Steinthal*, l. c.

Plato — 1. ὄνομα and 2. ῥῆμα; cf. *Classen*, l. c., pp. 43-52.

Aristotle (and Theodectes) — 1. ὄνομα, 2. ῥῆμα, 3. ἄρθρον 'article,' 4. συνδεσμός 'conjunction,' ibid., p. 55 ff. According to *Dionysius*, De comp. verb. 2 (= *Quint.* I 4), the article was not as yet recognized by these as a separate part of speech, but see *Classen*, p. 59 f.

Stoics (Chrysippus) — 1. ὄνομα, 2. προσηγορία 'appellatio,' 'proper names,' 3. ῥῆμα, 4. συνδεσμός, 5. ἄρθρον 'article and pronoun,' 6. μεσότης (πανδέκτης) 'adverb' added by Antipater.

Aristarchus — 1. ὄνομα, 2. ῥῆμα, 3. ἀντωνυμία 'pronoun,' 4. ἐπίρρημα 'adverb,' 5. μετοχή 'participle,' 6. ἄρθρον, 7. συνδεσμός, 8. πρόθεσις 'preposition.' [1]

Cf. *Classen*; *Lersch*; *Steinthal*, vol. II; *Schömann*, ll. cc.; *R. Schmidt*, Stoicorum grammatica, Halle, 1839; *Th. Rumpel*, Casuslehre, Halle, 1845, pp. 1-70; *Ribbach*, De A. arte grammatica, Nürnberg, 1883.

---

[1] The ancients, accustomed to see in Homer the fountain of all wisdom, supposed these *eight* parts of speech to have been well known to him, citing in proof of this the following lines:

Iliad, I 185: αὐτὸς ἰὼν κλισίηνδε τὸ σὸν γέρας ὄφρ᾽ εὖ εἰδῇς.

Iliad, XXII 59: πρὸς δέ με τὸν δύστηνον ἔτι φρονέοντ᾽ ἐλέησον.

(5) *Analogia* (Aristarchus and his school) vs. *Anomalia* (Crates and the Stoics).
Cf. Lersch; Steinthal, I, 357-74 II, 71-159.

i. *Hermippos* ὁ Καλλιμάχειος, of Smyrna.
Βίοι περὶ τῶν ἐν παιδείᾳ λαμψάντων.
Of this voluminous work: περὶ τῶν νομοθετῶν, [περὶ δούλων,?] περὶ τῶν ἑπτὰ σοφῶν, περὶ Πυθαγόρου, περὶ Ἀριστοτέλους, περὶ Γοργίου, περὶ Ἰσοκράτους, περὶ Ἰσοκράτους μαθητῶν, περὶ ἐνδόξων ἀνδρῶν ἰατρῶν, περὶ μάγων, περὶ τῶν ἀπὸ φιλοσοφίας εἰς τυραννίδας καὶ δυναστείας μεθεστηκότων — generally cited as separate books, formed only so many subdivisions. One of the chief sources of *Diogenes Laertius*, and of *Plutarch's* Lycurgus, Solon, Demosthenes, and indirectly, through the medium of Caecilius, of *Pseudo-Plutarch*, Vitae X oratorum. Cf. *Susemihl*, I, 492-95.

k. *Apollodorus of Athens* (pupil of Aristarchus), flor. c. 150. "Ἀπολλοδώρῳ περὶ πᾶσαν ἱστορίαν ἀνδρὶ δεινῷ" (*Ps. Heracl.* Alleg. Homer. 7).

(1) Χρονικά in comic trimeters, from the fall of Troy, (1184)-144 B.C. 2d. edition, to about 119 (death of Boethos the Academic mentioned). The inexhaustible storehouse of chronological information throughout antiquity. Calculation of the ἀκμή.
Cf. *Diels*, Rh. Mus. XXXI (1876), 1-54; also *G. F. Unger*, Philol., XL (1882), 602-51.

(2) Περὶ τοῦ νεῶν καταλόγου, 12 books. An exhaustive commentary to the Homeric Catalogue of the Ships.
Cf. *Niese*, Apollodor's Commentar zum Schiffscataloge als Quelle Strabo's, Rhein. Mus. XXXII (1877), 267-307.

(3) Περὶ Σώφρονος, 4 books.
(4) On *Epicharmus*, 10 books.

(5) Περὶ τῶν Ἀθήνησιν ἑταιρῶν.
(6) Περὶ ἐτυμολογιῶν.
(7) Περὶ θεῶν, 24 books. A work of stupendous erudition, freely and extensively pirated by later writers.

Cf. *Muenzel*, De Apollodori περὶ θεῶν libris, Bonn, 1883; and on A. in general cf. *Susemihl*, II, 33-44.

l. The first Manual of Mythology, written between 100–50 B.C., the source of *Diodorus, Hyginus, Pseudo-Apollodori* Bibliotheca, *Proclus*.

Cf. *Bethe*, Quaestiones Diodoreae mythographae, Göttingen, 1887, and *Hermes*, XXVI (1891), 593-634; *Susemihl*, II, 45-52.

m. Ammonius, pupil and successor of Aristarchus.

(1) Περὶ τοῦ μὴ γεγονέναι πλείονας (sc. τῶν δύο) ἐκδόσεις τῆς Ἀρισταρχείου διορθώσεως. See above under Aristarchus.
(2) Περὶ τῶν ὑπὸ Πλάτωνος μετενηνεγμένων ἐξ Ὁμήρου.
(3) Πρὸς Ἀθηνοκλέα σύγγραμμα.
(4) Commentary to *Pindar*.
(5) Κωμῳδούμενοι.
(6) Περὶ τῶν Ἀθήνησιν ἑταιρίδων.
(7) Περὶ προσῳδίας or Περὶ Ἀττικῆς προσῳδίας.

Cf. *Blau*, De Aristarchi discipulis, Jena, 1883; *A. Roemer*, Die Werke der Aristarcheer im Cod. Ven. A, Münch. Acad. II, 241 ff. (1875); *La Roche*, Hom. Textkritik, pp. 68-78; *Susemihl*, II, 153-155.

n. Dionysius Thrax of Alexandria, born c. 166 B.C.

(1) Τέχνη γραμματική, the first attempt of its kind and the standard work on the subject for more than 1500 years.

Cf. *Uhlig's* edition, with exhaustive Prolegomena, Lpz. 1883. For a list of *grammatical terms*, see below.

Of the numerous commentators of the τέχνη, *Choeroboscus* (6. cent.), *Stephanos* (7. cent.), *Helio-*

dorus, Melampus, Moschopulos are the most noteworthy.

Cf. *Hoerschelmann*, De Dionysii Thracis interpretibus veteribus I, Lpz. 1874, and especially *Hilgard*, Heidelberg Gymn. Progr. Lpz. 1880.

(2) Commentaries to the *Iliad* and *Odyssey* (28 frag.). Following Aristarchus, D. regarded Homer as an Athenian.

(3) Commentaries to *Hesiod's Works and Days*.

(4) Πρὸς Κράτητα.

(5) Περὶ ποσοτήτων.

(6) A work on *Rhetoric*.

(7) Μελέται.

Cf. *Mor. Schmidt*, Philol. VII, 360-82 VIII, 234-53. 510-20; *Susemihl*, II, 168-75. 687 f.

o. DIDYMUS CHALCENTEROS of Alexandria, c. 65 B.C.– c. 10 A.D.

Said to have written 3500-4000 books. *Amm. Marcell.* XXII 16, 16 Χαλκέντερος multiplicis scientiae copia memorabilis. *Quint.* I 8, 19, Didymo, quo nemo plura scripsit, accidisse compertum est, ut cum historiae cuidam tamquam vanae repugnaret, ipsius proferretur liber qui eam continebat. *Athen.* IV 139 : καλεῖ δὲ τοῦτον Δημήτριος ὁ Τροιζήνιος βιβλιολάθαν διὰ τὸ πλῆθος ὧν ἐκδέδωκε συγγραμμάτων · ἐστὶ γὰρ τρισχίλια πρὸς τοῖς πεντακοσίοις. *Macrob.* Sat. V 18, 9 ; grammaticorum facile eruditissimus. 22, 10 : grammaticorum omnium . . . instructissimus. Masterly discussion and estimate of D.'s work by *Wilamowitz*, Eur. Heracl. I, 157-68.

(l) *Lexicographical*.

(1) Διεφθορυῖα λέξις.

(2) Ἀπορουμένη λέξις, 7 books.

(3) Τροπικὴ λέξις.

(4) Κωμικὴ λέξις.
(5) Τραγικὴ λέξις.
} The chief source of the lexicographical erudition of the ancients preserved in lexica, scholia, Athenaeus, Hesychius, Photius, etc.

(6) Lexicon to Hippocrates (?).

(II) *Didymus as editor of texts and as commentator.*
  (1) Περὶ τῆς Ἀριστάρχου διορθώσεως. (Text and commentary to the Homeric poems.) See above.
  (2) Commentary to *Hesiod;* cf. *Schmidt,* pp. 299 f.
  (3) C. to *Pindar;* id., pp. 214–40.
  (4) C. to the *Epinikia* of *Bacchylides.*
  (5) C. to *Aeschylus, Sophocles, Euripides* (in part). The extant *vitae* are in all essential details Didymean. Prejudicial and partial criticism of Soph. to the disparagement of Euripides. Cf. *A. Roemer* (cited below).
  (6) C. to *Ion* and perhaps to *Achaeos;* cf. *Schmidt,* pp. 301–5.
  (7) C. to *Cratinus* and *Eupolis; Schmidt,* pp. 307–9.
  (8) C. to *Aristophanes; Schmidt,* pp. 246–61; *Schneider,* De fontibus A. schol., pp. 59–63. [Aristophanes of Byz.—Didymus—Symmachus—extant scholia.]
  (9) C. to *Menander* and to *Phrynichus* (Kronos); *Schmidt,* pp. 306 ff.
  (10) Editions and Commentaries to *Antiphon, Isaeus, Hypereides, Aeschines* and *Demosthenes — Schmidt,* pp. 310–19 — *Isocrates* (?), *Deinarchus* (?).
  (11) Edition of *Thucydides.* The extant life by *Marcellinus* (esp. § 1–45) was almost entirely taken from Didymus' introduction. Cf. *Susemihl,* II, 203 f., note 314.
  (12) Ῥητορικὰ ὑπομνήματα, in at least 10 books; *Schmidt,* p. 321. Exegetical parerga to the *Attic orators.*

(13) Περὶ τοῦ δεκατεῦσαι; *Schmidt*, pp. 317 f.
(III) *Grammatical works:*
  (1) Περὶ παθῶν (on inflections); *Schmidt*, pp. 343 ff.
  (2) Περὶ ὀρθογραφίας.
  (3) Περὶ τῆς παρὰ Ῥωμαίοις ἀναλογίας. Doubtful.
(IV) *Historical, antiquarian, literary treatises:*
  (1) Ξένη ἱστορία; cf. *Schmidt*, pp. 356–63.
  (2) *De morte Aeneae;* ⎫
  (3) *De patria Homeri;* ⎬ cf. *Schmidt*,
  (4) *On Anacreon and Sappho;* ⎭ pp. 384–6.
  Cf. *Seneca*, Ep. 88, 37 : quatuor milia librorum Didymus grammaticus scripsit . . . in his libris de patria Homeri quaeritur, in his de Aeneae morte (matre, MSS.) vera, in his libidinosior Anacreon an ebriosior vixerit, in his an Sappho publica fuerit.
  (5) Περὶ ποιητῶν; *Schmidt*, pp. 386–96.
  (6) Πρὸς Ἴωνα (?) ἀντεξηγήσεις. (A long extract on the musical instruments used in lyric poetry preserved by *Athen.* XIV 634 *e.*) Perhaps a part of (5).
  (7) Περὶ τῶν ἀξόνων τῶν Σόλωνος ἀντιγραφὴ πρὸς Ἀσκληπιάδην (*Plut.* Sol. 1).
  (8) *Against Cicero's de Republica,* 6 books. Cf. *Amm. Marcell.* XXII 16, 16, and *Suidas* s. v. Τράγκυλλος.
  (9) Περὶ παροιμιῶν.
  (10) *On the city of Kabassos* and on *Attic demes* (doubtful). Perhaps portions of his commentaries to the Iliad (13, 363) or to the comic poets or to the Attic orators.
  Cf. *Mor. Schmidt*, Didymi Chalcenteri grammatici Alexandrini fragmenta, Lpz. 1854; *Ludwig*, l. c.; *Susemihl*, II, 195–210. 688 f.

p. Tryphon of Alexandria, son of Ammonius.
  A specialist on Greek grammar. A confused list of his numerous works is given by *Suidas,* the titles

of others are cited by Apollonius Dyscolos, Herodianus, Athenaeus.

(1) Περὶ πλεονασμοῦ, περὶ μέτρων, περὶ τρόπων, περὶ σχημάτων.

(2) On the dialects of Greece, on the dialect of Homer and the lyric poets.

(3) Περὶ Ἀττικῆς προσῳδίας, περὶ ὀνομασιῶν, περὶ ὀρθογραφίας καὶ τῶν ἐν αὐτῇ ζητουμένων (= its problems), περὶ Ἑλληνισμοῦ (on idiomatic speech), περὶ ἀρχαίας ἀναγνώσεως (on style).

(4) Περὶ πνευμάτων, περὶ τῆς ἐν μονοσυλλάβοις ἀναλογίας, περὶ τῆς ἐν κλίσεσιν (declensions) ἀναλογίας, περὶ ἄρθρων, περὶ ἀντωνυμιῶν (pronouns), περὶ προσώπων (persons), περὶ μετοχῆς (participle), περὶ προθέσεων (prepositions), περὶ συνδεσμῶν, περὶ ἐπιρρημάτων (adverbs), περὶ ῥημάτων ἐγκλιτικῶν (moods), περὶ ῥημάτων ἀναλογίας βαρυτόνων, περὶ ὀνομάτων συγκριτικῶν (comparison of adjectives), περὶ παθῶν λέξεων (inflections).

(5) Φυτῶν ἱστορία, περὶ ζώων.

Cf. *A. v. Velsen*, Tryphonis grammatici Alexandrini fragmenta, Berlin, 1854; *Susemihl*, II, 210–13. 689.

q. Theon of Alexandria, 1. cent. A.D.

"The Didymus of the Alexandrian poets."

(1) Commentaries to *Lycophron, Theocritus, Callimachus'* Αἴτια, *Apollonius Rhodius, Nicandros*.

(2) Commentary to the *Odyssey* and perhaps to *Pindar*.

(3) Λέξις κωμική.

(4) Λέξις τραγική (doubtful, but probable).

Cf. *Giese*, De Theone grammatico eiusque reliquiis, Münster, Diss., 1867; *Wilamowitz*, Eur. Heracl. I, 156; *Susemihl*, II, 216 ff.

3. THE STOICS AS PHILOLOGIANS.

Allegorical exegesis of Homer. Contributions to the Science and Terminology of Grammar.

Cf. *Gräfenhan*, 1. c., I, 440 ff. 505 ff. II, 23. III, 236; *R. Schmidt*, De Stoicorum grammatica, Halle, 1839; *Steinthal*, 1. c.; *Stricker*, De Stoicorum studiis rhetoricis, Bresl. Abh. I 2 (1886).

a. *Chrysippos* of Soli, c. 280–c. 206. Wrote e.g. περὶ τῆς κατὰ τὰς λέξεις ἀνωμαλίας (the first occurrence of the term), λόγοι παρὰ τὰς συνηθείας, κατὰ τῆς συνηθείας, περὶ τῆς συνηθείας, περὶ πέντε πτώσεων, περὶ ὁμονοίας (*Athen.* VI 267) περὶ ἑνικῶν καὶ πληθυντικῶν ἐκφορῶν, περὶ τῆς ῥητορικῆς, περὶ τῶν στοιχείων τοῦ λόγου καὶ τῶν λεγομένων, πῶς δεῖ τῶν ποιημάσων ἀκούειν (source of Plutarch's treatise of the same title).

Cf. *Aronis*, Χρύσιππος γραμματικός, Diss. Iena 1885. For a full list of his works, see *Laert. Diog.* VII 190 ff.

b. *Crates of Mallos* (flor. 168 B.C.) *and the School of Pergamum.*

A follower of the Stoics. Passionate opponent of Aristarchus and his school (*Suidas* s. v. Ἀρίσταρχος : καὶ Κρὰτητι τῷ γραμματικῷ πλεῖστα διημιλλήσατο). *Bibaculus* ap. *Sueton.* de gramm. 110. En iecur Cratetis. Advocate of ἀνωμαλία vs. ἀναλογία.

Cf. the bibliography under Aristarchus and below.

Introduced *philological studies into Rome;* cf. *Sueton.*, 1. c., p. 100.

(1) *Homer.*

a. Διόρθωσις (Διορθωτικά), critical edition, probably with the Life of Homer.

b. Ὁμηρικά, allegorical commentary.

c. Περὶ Ἰλιάδος καὶ Ὀδυσσείας (ὑπομνήματα or συγγράμματα?).

Cf. *E. Maass*, Aratea pp. 167–203.

(2) Commentary to *Hesiod, Works and Days.*

(3) C. to *Euripides* (Schol. Orest. 1226. 1686; Phoen. 208 Rhesus, 5. 528 f.).

Cf. *Wilamowitz*, Anal. Eurip., p. 157.

(4) C. to *Aristophanes* (Schol. Equit. 631, 793, 693; Vesp. 352. 884 Ran. 294).

Cf. *Consbruch*, Zu den Tractaten περὶ κωμῳδίας in Comment. in honor. Studemundi, Strassburg, 1889; *Susemihl*, II, 11, note 54.

(5) Περὶ Ἀττικῆς διαλέκτου, in at least 5 books.

Cf. in general, *Wegener*, De aula Attalica, 1836 (antiquated); *Wachsmuth*, De Cratete Mallota, Lpz. 1860, with fragments; id., Philol. XVI, 166; Rhein. Mus. XLVI, 552-56; *Lübbert*, Rhein. Mus. XI, 428-43; *Susemihl*, II, iv f. 4-12. 703; *A. Conze*, Berl. Acad. Sitzungsber. 1884, pp. 1259 ff.

c. *Demetrius Magnes* (contemporary of Cicero).

(1) Περὶ συνωνύμων πόλεων.

(2) Περὶ τῶν συνωνύμων ποιητῶν τε καὶ συγγραφέων. Chapter on *Deinarchus* preserved by *Dionys. Halic.* de Deinarch. One of the chief sources of *Diogenes Laertius*.

Cf. *Nietzsche*, Rhein. Mus. XXIII, 632-53 XXIV, 181-228; *Scheurleer*, De D. M., Leiden, 1858; *Maass*, Philol. Unters. III (1880), 23-47; *Susemihl*, I, 507 f.

II. THE GRAECO-ROMAN PERIOD.

1. THE POST-ALEXANDRIAN PERIOD.

a. *Dionysius of Halicarnassus* (flor. end of 1. cent. B.C.).

(1) Epistula ad Ammaeum I.
(2) De compositione verborum.
(3) De oratoribus antiquis (Lysias, Isocrates, Isaeus, Demosth.), De Dinarcho.
(4) Epistula ad Pompeium.
(5) Περὶ μιμήσεως γ'.
(6) De Thucydide.
(7) Ad Ammaeum II.
(8) [Ars rhetorica.]

Cf. *Fr. Blass*, De D. H. scriptis rhetoricis, Bonn, 1863; *Rössler*, De D. H. scriptis rhetor., Lpz. 1873; *H. Usener*, D. H. de imitatione reliquiae, Bonn, 1889; *E. Egger*, l. c., pp. 396-406. *G. Ammon*, De D. H. rhet. fontibus, Munich Diss. 1889, pp. 110.

b. Caecilius Calactinus (Friend of Dionysius).
(1) Περὶ τοῦ χαρακτῆρος τῶν δέκα ῥητόρων. Chief source of *Ps. Plut.* Vitae X orat. On the canon of the ten orators, see under *Aristophanes*.
(2) Comparison between Demosth. and Aesch., Demosth. and Cicero.
(3) Περὶ ὕψους (cf. Ps. Longinus, Περὶ ὕψους 1).
(4) Ἐκλογὴ λέξεων κατὰ στοιχεῖον (καλλιρρημοσύνη).
(5) Τέχνη ῥητορική.
(6) Περὶ σχημάτων.

On Dionysius and Caecilius, the most noteworthy representatives of literary criticism in antiquity, cf. *F. Blass*, Gesch. der griech. Beredsamkeit von Alexander bis auf Augustus, Berlin, 1865, pp. 169–221. *R. Weise*, Quaest. Caecil. Berlin 1888, pp. 52.

c. Διονυσίου ἢ Λογγίνου Περὶ ὕψους (composed in the 1 cent. A.D.). Aesthetic and Literary Criticism.

Cf. *Buchenau*, De scriptore libri Περὶ ὕψους, Marb. 1849; *Martens*, De libello Περὶ ὕψους, Bonn, 1877; *Egger*, 1. c., pp. 426–39; *Coblentz*, De libelli Περὶ ὕψους auctore, Strassb. Diss. 1888 pp. 76; *Ph. Caccialanza*, in Riv. di Filologia XVIII (1889), 2–73.

d. APOLLONIOS DYSCOLOS, ὁ τεχνικός (2 cent. A.D.).
Founder of scientific syntax. "Σύνταξις ἀναγκαιοτάτη πρὸς ἐξήγησιν τῶν ποιημάτων." "Maximus auctor artis grammaticae" *Priscian*.
(1) Ὀνοματικόν (declension).
(2) Ῥηματικόν (conjugation).
(3) Περὶ ἀντωνυμίας ⎫
(4) Περὶ ἐπιρρημάτων ⎬ extant   μέρη τοῦ λόγου.
(5) Περὶ συνδέσμων ⎭
(6) Περὶ συντάξεως, 4 bks., extant.

Cf. *Gräfenhan*, III, 109 ff.; *L. Lange*, Das System der Syntax des A.D., Göttingen, 1852; *E. Egger*, A.D., Essai sur l'histoire des théories grammaticales dans l'antiquité, Paris, 1854, pp. 354; *Steinthal*, II, 220–345.

c. AELIUS HERODIANUS (son of A. D.).
The greatest grammarian of antiquity.
(1) Καθολικὴ προσῳδία, in 21 books.
  α. Bks. 1-19 — προσῳδίαι, τόνοι.
  β. Bk. 20 — χρόνοι ('quantity').
  γ. Bk. 21 — On accents, enclitics, diastole, synaloephe. Excerpts preserved by *Theodosius* and *Arcadius*.
(2) Περὶ ὀρθογραφίας, περὶ παθῶν, περὶ ὀνομάτων, περὶ κλίσεως ὀνομάτων, περὶ ῥημάτων, περὶ συζυγιῶν ('conjugations'), περὶ βαρβαρισμοῦ, περὶ μονοσυλλάβων. Originals all lost; contents known through excerpts in later grammarians.
(3) Περὶ μονήρους λέξεως (on peculiar, anomalous grammatical forms). Extant.

Cf. *Aug. Lentz*, Herodiani technici reliquiae, 2 vols., Lpz. 1870 (ccxxviii+564, vii+1264, with indexes); *Lehrs*, Herodiani scripta tria, Königsberg, 1848; *Pauly, R. E.*, III, 1236-40; *E. Hiller*, Jahrb. f. Philol. 118 (1871), 505-32. 603-29, Quaest. Herodianae, Bonn, 1866.

f. EPITOMATORS, LEXICOGRAPHERS.
  a. *Iuba*, king of Mauretania, "ἁπάντων ἱστορικώτατος βασιλέων," *Plut*. Sertor. c. 9. Author of the θεατρικὴ ἱστορία, one of the sources of Pollux.

Cf. *Rohde*, De Pollucis fontibus, Lpz. 1870; *Bapp*, Lpz. Stud. VIII, 110 ff.

  β. *Pamphilus*, Περὶ γλωσσῶν ἤτοι λέξεων (Λειμών). 95 bks.
  Epitomized by *Vestinus* and by *Diogenianus* in 5 bks.

Cf. *Weber*, Philol. Suppl. III, 467 ff.

  γ. HERENNIOS PHILON of Byblos (61-141 A.D.).
    (1) Περὶ κτήσεως καὶ ἐκλογῆς βιβλίων, 12 bks.
    (2) Περὶ πόλεων καὶ οὓς ἑκάστη αὐτῶν ἐνδόξους ἤνεγκεν, in 30 bks. A famous compilation

most extensively used by later grammarians, esp. Hesychius and Stephanus Byzantius.

Cf. *Daub*, Jahrb. f. Phil. Suppl. XI 437 ff.

δ. *Hephaestion* (older contemporary of Athenaeus).

Athen. XV p. 673 e : 'Λαβὼν δὲ παρ' ἐμοῦ ὁ πᾶσιν κλοπὴν ὀνειδίζων Ἡφαιστίων ἐξιδιοποιήσατο τὴν λύσιν.' Chief work : Περὶ μέτρων. 48 bks. (lost). His own epitome, Ἐγχειρίδιον περὶ μέτρων, in 1 bk. (cf. *Longin.* Proleg. ad Hephaest. p. 88, 21) became the standard school-book throughout later antiquity and the Middle Ages.

Cf. *Westphal*, Metrik der Griechen, Vol. I, introduction.

ε. *Athenaeus* of Naucratis (close of 2. cent. A.D.).

On the sources of the Δειπνοσοφισταί (in 15 bks.) cf. *K. Bapp*, Leipz. Studien VIII, 85–160, *F. Rudolph*, Philologus Suppl. Vol. VI 1, pp. 109–163.

ζ. *Aelius Dionysius and Pausanias*, Ἀττικισταί.

Cf. *Rindfleisch*, De P. et D. lexicis rhetoricis, Königsberg, 1866. *H. Heyden*, Quaest. de Ael. D. et P. Atticistis, Etym. Magn. fontibus in Leipz. Stud. VIII 2 (1886), pp. 173–264; Ael. D. et P. Atticistis fragm. coll. *E. Schwabe*, Leipz. 1890 pp. 282 (Prolegom. 1–80).

η. *Valerius Harpocration* (2. cent.).

Λέξεις τῶν δέκα ῥητόρων.

Based upon very valuable sources now lost. Cf. *Boysen*, De Harpocratiae fontibus, Kiel, 1876.

θ. *Julius Pollux* (Πολυδεύκης) of *Naucratis*.

Ὀνομαστικόν in 10 bks. Cf. *Rohde*, l. c.

ι. *Cassius Longinus* (†270–275).

'Βιβλιοθήκη ἔμψυχος καὶ περιπατοῦν μουσεῖον,' Eunapios. 'Φιλόλογος μὲν ὁ Λογγῖνος, φιλόσοφος δὲ μηδαμῶς,' Porphyrius. Pupil of Plotinus, teacher of Porphyrius. ὁ κριτικός (*Suidas* s. v. Φρόντων).

(1) Φιλόλογοι ὁμιλίαι, in at least 21 bks.; fragm.

(2) Ἀττικῶν λέξεων ἐκδόσεις.
(3) Ἀπορήματα Ὁμηρικά, Προβλήματα Ὁμήρου καὶ λύσεις, εἰ φιλόσοφος Ὅμηρος. } lost.
(4) Rhetoric (ἀφορμαὶ λόγου) discovered by Ruhnken amid the Rhetoric of Apsines.

Cf. *Walz*, Rhet. Graec. IX p. xxiii ff.

(5) [Περὶ ὕψους] falsely ascribed to Longinus; cf. above.

Cf. *D. Ruhnken*, De vita et scriptis Longini, 1776; *E. Egger*, pp. 475-84.

LIST OF THE MOST IMPORTANT, EXTANT SCHOLIA.

Cf. *E. Hübner*, Encyclopaedie, pp. 37-40^2; *Wilamowitz*, Eur. Her. I, 173-210.

1. *Homer.*
Subscriptio in the cod. Ven. A : Παράκειται τὰ Ἀριστονίκου σημεῖα καὶ Διδύμου περὶ Ἀρισταρχείου διορθώσεως, τινὰ δὲ καὶ ἐκ τῆς Ἰλιαδῆς προσῳδίας Ἡρωδιανοῦ καὶ ἐκ τῶν Νικάνορος περὶ στιγμῆς. "Viermänner Scholien," cf. above.

Cf. *Ludwig*, l. c., *Friedländer*, Aristonicus, 1853; id., Nicanor, 1850; *Fabricius*, Bibl. Gr. I, 440-56 (index auctorum).

2. *Aristophanes.*
Subscriptio to the Clouds and Wasps : κεκώλισται ἐκ τοῦ Ἡλιοδώρου, παραγέγραπται ἐκ τοῦ Φαεινοῦ καὶ Συμμάχου καὶ ἄλλων τινῶν.

Cf. *O. Schneider*, De Veterum in Arist. scholiorum fontibus, 1838; *Wilamowitz*, Eur. Her. I, 179-84; *W. Meiners*, Quaest. ad scholia Λ. hist. pertinentes, in Diss. Hallens. XI, 217-403; *Fabricius*, II, 392-404 (index auctorum).

3. *Apollonius Rhodius.*
Subscriptio in the Cod. Mediceus : Παράκειται τὰ σχόλια ἐκ τῶν Λουκίλλου Ταρραίου καὶ Σοφοκλέους καὶ Θέωνος.

Cf. *Weichert*, Apollon. Rhod. pp. 400 ff.; *Bernhardy*, Griech. Literat. II 1, pp. 370 ff.; *Susemihl*, I, 662 II, 46. 686; *Fabricius* IV, 279-86 (index auctorum).

4. *Pindar.*
   Cf. *K. Lehrs*, Die Pindarscholien, Lpz. 1863; *Fabricius* II, 81-4.
5. *Aeschylus.*
   J. Richter, De Aesch. Soph. Eur. interpretibus Graecis, Berlin, 1839.
6. *Sophocles.*
   Bernhardy, l. c. II 2, pp. 378 ff.
7. *Euripides.*
   Bernhardy, l. c. II 2, pp. 498 ff.
8. *Theocritos; Nicandros; Aratus; Callimachus'* Hymns.
9. *Lycophron.* (*I. Tzetzes.*)
10. *Plato.*
    L. Cohn, J. J. Suppl. XIII, 773. *Th. Mettauer*, De Platonis scholiorum fontibus, Zürich, 1880 (pp. 122).
11. *Aristotle.* Commentaries of Alexander of Aphrodisias, Simplicius, Philoponus.
12. *Demosthenes.*

CRITICAL SIGNS (Σημεῖα, notae).

Cf. *Reifferscheid*, Suetonii Reliquiae, pp. 137-44.

Ὀβελός (—). — 'πρὸς τὰ νόθα καὶ ἀθετούμενα.' Legendary origin of name, l. c. p. 138.

Διπλῆ ἀπερίστικτος, καθαρά (>). — 'παράκειται : 1. πρὸς τὴν ἅπαξ εἰρημένην λέξιν 2. πρὸς τὴν τοῦ ποιητοῦ συνήθειαν (inconsistency) 3. πρὸς τοὺς λέγοντας, μὴ εἶναι τοῦ αὐτοῦ ποιητοῦ Ἰλιάδα καὶ Ὀδύσσειαν (χωρίζοντες) 4. πρὸς τὰς τῶν παλαιῶν ἱστορίας 5. πρὸς τὰς τῶν νέων ἐνδοχάς 6. πρὸς τὴν Ἀττικὴν σύνταξιν 7. πρὸς τὴν πολύσημον λέξιν.' 'Usus est ea in multis *Aristarchus*, nunc ea quae praeter consuetudinem tam vitae nostrae quam ipsius poetae apud eum invenirentur adnotans, nunc proprias ipsius figuras, interdum ea in quibus copiosus est, rursus quae semel apud

eum ponerentur. Similiter in nostris auctoribus *Probus*.'
'Primus Leogoras Syracusanus apposuit Homericis versibus ad separationem Olympi a caelo.'

Διπλῆ περιεστιγμένη (>). — 'πρὸς τὰς γραφὰς τὰς Ζηνοδοτείους καὶ Κράτητος καὶ αὐτοῦ Ἀριστάρχου καὶ τὰς διορθώσεις αὐτοῦ.'

Ἀστερίσκος καθ' ἑαυτόν (※).—'πρὸς τοὺς αὐτοὺς στίχους οἳ κεῖνται ἐν ἄλλοις μέρεσιν τῆς ποιήσεως, καὶ ὀρθῶς ἔχοντες φέρονται, σημαίνων ὅτι οὗτοι καὶ ἀλλαχοῦ εἴρηνται. 'Aristophanes apponebat illis locis quibus sensus deesset, Aristarchus autem ad eos [versus] qui hoc puta loco [recte] positi erant, cum aliis scilicet non recte ponerentur, item Probus et antiqui nostri.' Cf. however schol. γ 71.

Ἀστερίσκος μετ' ὀβελοῦ (※—). — 'ἔνθα εἰσὶ μὲν τὰ ἔπη τοῦ ποιητοῦ οὐ καλῶς δὲ κεῖνται, ἀλλ' ἐν ἄλλῳ.' 'Propria est nota Aristarchi, utebatur autem ea in his versibus qui non suo loco positi sunt, item Probus et antiqui nostri.' Cf. e.g. A 195.

Ἀντίσιγμα (Ɔ). — 'πρὸς τοὺς ἐνηλλαγμένους τόπους καὶ μὴ συνᾴδοντας.' 'Ponebatur ad eos versus quorum ordo permutandus erat.'

Ἀντίσιγμα περιεστιγμένον (·Ɔ·). —'ὅταν δύο ὦσι διάνοιαι τὸ αὐτὸ σημαίνουσαι(ταυτολογεῖ), τοῦ ποιητοῦ γεγραφότος ἀμφοτέρας, ὅπως τὴν ἑτέραν ἕληται.' σίγμα—Aristoph.=στιγμή— Aristarch. Cf. B 192.

Κεραύνιον (Ꞇ) — Rare. — 'δηλοῖ πολλὰς ζητήσεις πρὸς ταῖς προειρημέναις.' 'Ponitur quotiens multi versus improbantur ne per singulos obelentur.'

X (in scholia to tragedians).

Ancient authorities: Aristonicus (see above), *Diogenianos* (?) περὶ τῶν ἐν τοῖς βιβλίοις σημείων (Suid.), *Diog. Laert.* III 65, *Suetonius = Isidorus*, Origg. I, 21 ff., de notis scripturarum. See below. *Anecd. Roman.* ed. Osann, *Anecd. Venetum*, ed. Villoison, *Anecd. Paris.* ed. Cramer (all collected in Reifferscheid l. c.).

Modern treatises: Gräfenhan II, 92 f.; *Sengebusch,* Hom. Diss. I, 22 ff.; *Nauck,* Aristoph. Byzant. pp. 17 ff.; *Ludwig,* I, 20 ff.; *Susemihl,* I, 432 ff.; *H. Schrader,* De notatione critica a veteribus grammaticis in poetis scaenicis adhibita, Bonn, 1863; and *A. Roemer,* Die Notation der Alexand. Philol. bei d. griech. Dramat. in Bayr. Acad. Cl. I Vol. XIX, pt. III, 1-52 (1892).

Principal Grammatical Terms.

GREEK.

I. Ὄνομα (Noun).
 1. Γένος: ἄρρενα θήλεα, σκεύη (οὐδέτερον — Stoics). Cf. *Arist.* Rhet. III 5 Πρωταγόρας τὰ γένη τῶν ὀνομάτων διῄρει *Soph.* Elench. 14. Alexandrian scholars added κοινόν (ὁ ἡ βοῦς), ἐπίκοινον (ὁ ἀετός).
 2. Ἀριθμός: ἑνικός, πληθυντικός, and δυϊκός (added by Zenodotus?).
 3. Κλίσεις (declension).
    a. ὀνομαστική, εὐθεῖα, ὀρθή
    b. γενική, also πατρική and κτητική (possessive)
    c. δοτική
    d. αἰτιατική, also ἐπισταλτική
    e. κλητική, also προσαγορευτική

    ⎫
    ⎪
    ⎬ (πτώσεις cases).
    ⎪
    ⎭

    Πτώσεις πλαγίαι, ὑπτίαι (oblique cases).
    These terms were still unknown to *Aristotle,* for in Anal. Prior. I, 36 he declines a masc., fem. and neuter noun in full.

II. Ῥῆμα (Verb).
 1. Συζυγίαι (conjugation). In Dionysius Thrax still divided according to accent.
 2. Διαθέσεις (Voices).
    Arist. Categ. 4 Soph. Elench. 4: ποιεῖν, πάσχειν (ἐνέργεια, πάθος).
    Stoics: ὀρθόν (active), ὕπτιον (passive), οὐδέτερον (intransitive middle), μέση (middle).
    Dionysius Thrax: ἐνέργεια, πάθος, μεσότης.

Later: ἐνεργητική, παθητική, μεσότης (which latter, however, also includes the 2*d. perfect*).

3. Ἐγκλίσεις (Moods), πτώσεις ῥηματικαί (*Dionys.* de comp. verb. 6).

Protagoras: ἐντολή (imperative), εὐχωλή (optative), ἀπόκρισις (indicative), ἐρώτησις (subjunctive) — Πυθμένες λόγου.

Dionysius Thrax: a. ὁριστική (indic., so called because all definitions, ὅροι, were in this mood) b. προστατική (imperative) c. εὐκτική (optative) d. ὑποτακτική (subjunctive) e. ἀπαρέμφατος (infinitive).

4. Χρόνοι (Tenses).

Cf. *Plat.* Soph. 262 c. περὶ τῶν ὄντων ἢ γιγνομένων ἢ γεγονότων ἢ μελλόντων. (This double present was not accepted by later grammarians). *Arist.* Top. II 4 τὸ μὲν γὰρ τοῦ παρεληλυθότος χρόνου ἐστί, τὸ δὲ καὶ τοῦ παρόντος καὶ τοῦ μέλλοντος. *Stoics:* ἐνεστῶτα, παρωχηκότα, μέλλοντα.

Dionysius: χρόνοι δὲ τρεῖς : ἐνεστώς, παρεληλυθώς, μέλλων. τούτων ὁ παρεληλυθώς ἔχει διαφορὰς τέσσαρας : παρατακτικόν (imperfect), παρακείμενον (τέλειος, perfect), ὑποσυντελικόν (ὑπερτέλειος, pluperfect), ἀόριστον.

5. Πρόσωπα (Persons) : πρῶτον, δεύτερον, τρίτον.

Cf. *Lersch*, Sprachphilos. II, 170–222 ; *Steinthal*, Gesch. der Sprachwiss. II, 209–306. On the terminology of the parts of speech, see above under Aristarchus.

ROMAN.

The Latin terminology of grammar, so far as it is independent of the Greek, seems to have been chiefly due to *Varro* and *Nigidius Figulus*, but their nomenclature was not accepted by later scholars, translations from the Greek being preferred.

I. **Nomen** (Substantivum).
   1. Genus : *virile, muliebre, commune, promiscuum.* The terms '*masculinum*' and '*femininum*' cannot now be traced back farther than to *Caesellius Vindex* (2d. cent. A.D. Cf. *Gell.* N. A. VI (VII), 2), though they doubtless arose much earlier.
   2. Numerus : *singularis species, multitudinis species* (*Varro*), *plurativus* (*e.g. Gell.* I 16, XIX 8), *pluralis* (*e.g. Quint.* I 5, 16).
   3. Casus:
      a. rectus, *nominativus.*
      b. casus interrogandi (*Nigidius*), patricus (*Varro*), paternus, possessivus, *genetivus.*
      c. casus dandi (*Nigidius, Varro*), *dativus.*
      d. casus accusandei (*Varro*), *accusativus* — a false translation of αἰτιατική = causativus, which is also occasionally found.
      e. casus vocandei (*Varro*), salutatorius, *vocativus.*
      f. Sextus or Latinus casus (*Varro*), *ablativus* — probably introduced by Caesar in his De Analogia. Casus *recti* and *obliqui*. (See above.)
II. **Verbum.**
   1. Coniugatio, ordo. The *four* conjugations seem to be post-Varronian.
   2. Genera, adfectus, significatio : *activum, passivum, neutra, communis, deponens.*
   3. Modi, qualitates, status, inclinatio : a. *finitus, indicativus* b. *imperativus* c. *optativus* d. *subiunctivus* e. *infinitus, infinitivus.*
   4. Tempora : *praesens, praeteritum, futurum,* praeteritum imperfectum, praet. perfectum, plusquamperfectum.
   5. Personae. As above.

   Cf. *Lersch* op. cit. pp. 223–256; *L. Ieep,* Zur Gesch. von d. Redetheilen bei den Alten, pp. 124–259.

2. Roman Period.

Bibliography: Suetonius, de grammat. et rhetor.; *W. H. D. Suringar*, Historia Critica scholiastarum Latinorum, 3 vols., Leyden, 1835; *Gräfenhan*, II, 261 ff. IV; *Teuffel-Schwabe*, Röm. Literat. 2 vols. 1890⁵ ⟨T. S.⟩ § 41: *H. Nettleship*, Journ. of Phil. XV, 189 ff.

a. L. Accius, 170–c. 86.

Didascalica (cf. Aristotle's Διδασκαλίαι). A history of Greek and Roman poetry, with special reference to the drama. Orthographical reforms. Written chiefly in Sotadean verse.

Cf. *T. S.* § 134, 7, and 94, 2. *O. Ribbeck*, Röm. Dichtkunst, I, 267; *G. Hermann*, Opusc. VIII, 390 ff.; *Lachmann*, Kl. Schr. II, 67 ff.; *Madvig*, Opusc. Acad. 70 ff., *Fr. Ritschl*, Opusc. IV, 142 ff.

b. L. Aelius Praeconinus Stilo, flor. c. 100 B.C.

The *first* Roman philologian, teacher of Cicero and Varro. *Cic.* Brut. 205: eruditissimus et Graecis litteris et Latinis antiquitatisque nostrae et in inventis rebus et in actis scriptorumque veterum litterate peritus, quam scientiam Varro noster acceptam ab illo. *Varro ap. Gell.* N. A., I 18, 2: litteris ornatissimus memoria nostra, *id.* X 21, 2 doctissimus eorum temporum.

(1) Commentaries to *Carmina Saliorum*, cf. *Suringar* I, 26 f.

(2) Interpretation of the *XII Tables. Suringar* I, 39 ff.

(3) Edition of *Plautus* with critical signs.

Gell. N. A., III 3, 12: L. Aelius XXV (comoedias) eius (Plauti) esse solas existimavit; *Quint.* X 1, 99, "Licet Varro Musas, Aeli Stilonis sententia, Plautino dicat sermone locuturas fuisse, si Latine loqui vellent." Cf. *Ritschl*, Parerga 91 ff. 126 f. 238. 366.

(4) Contributions to *etymology* and *grammar*.

Cf. *T. S.* § 148, 1. *F. Mentz,* De L. Aelio Stilone, Diss. Ienens, IV 1.

c. *M. Tullius Cicero,* 106–43.

(1) Literary or aesthetic criticism.

Cf. *Ch. Causeret,* Sur la langue de la rhétorique et de la critique littéraire en Cic., Paris, 1887; *I. Kubik,* De Cic. poetarum lat. studiis, Diss. Vindob. I, 237 ff.

(2) Edition (?) of *Lucretius.*

Cf. *Munro,* Lucretius, vol. II, 2 ff.; *T. S.* § 203, 2.

d. *C. Iulius Caesar,* 100–44.

De analogia (Suet. Caes. c. 56).

Cf. *F. Schlitte,* De C. Iulio Caesare grammatico, Halle, 1865.

e. M. TERENTIUS VARRO *Reatinus,* 116–27.

'Vir Romanorum eruditissimus' (*Quint.* X 1, 95).

'Vir doctissimus undicumque Varro, qui tam multa legit ut aliquid ei scribere vacasse miremur, tam multa scripsit (620 bks.) quam vix quemquam legere potuisse credamus'(*Augustin.,* Civ. Dei. 6, 2). *Plut.* Rom. 12 ἄνδρα Ῥωμαίων ἐν ἱστορίᾳ βιβλιακώτατον. Esp. *Cic.* Acad. post. 1, 9.

Cf. *Ritschl,* Die Schriftstellerei des Varro in Opusc. III, 419–505, Parerga, pp. 70 ff.; *G. Boissier,* M. T. Varron, sa vie et ses ouvrages, Paris, 1861, pp. 337. *T. S.* § 166 f.

(1) *Antiquitatum libri* XLI.

(2) Annalium libri III — De vita populi Romani (cp. Dicaearchos Βίος Ἑλλάδος); De gente populi Romani, in 4 bks. (43 B.C.); de familiis Troianis; Aetia (cp. Αἴτια of Callimachus); rerum urbanarum libri III; Tribuum liber.

(3) De bibliothecis libri III: de proprietate scriptorum; *de poetis; de poematis;* de lectionibus; de compositione saturarum; de originibus scaenicis; de scaenicis actionibus; de actis scaenicis (Didascalica); de personis (masks); de descriptionibus; *quaestiones Plautinae; de comoediis Plautinis.*

(4) Disciplinarum libri IX (Artes liberales : 1. grammatica ; 2. dialectica ; 3. rhetorica ; 4. geometria ; 5. arithmetica ; 6. astrologia ; 7. musica ; 8. medicina ; 9. architectura).

(5) *De Lingua Latina*, XXV lbb. (V–X extant).
V–XXV, dedicated to Cicero, hence published before 43 B.C. *Contents:* Bk. I (introd.), bk. II–VII (etymology), VIII–XVI (inflection, analogy and anomaly), XVII–XXV (syntax).

(6) De sermone Latino libb. V ; de similitudine verborum libb. III (analogy) ; de utilitate sermonis ; περὶ χαρακτήρων (?=descriptiones) ; de antiquitate litterarum ; de origine linguae Latinae.

Cf. *Wilmanns*, de M. T. V. libris grammaticis, Berlin, 1864.

f. P. Nigidius Figulus († 45 B.C.). Homo, ut ego arbitror, iuxta M. Varronem doctissimus (*Gell.* N. A. IV 9, 1) ; vir doctrina et eruditione studiorum praestantissimus (*Schol. Bob.* to Cic. Vatin. p. 317 Or.).

Chief philological work : *Commentarii grammatici* in about 30 bks. Dealt also with orthography, synonymics and etymology. Frequently cited by *Gellius*.

Cf. *M. Hertz*, de N. F. studiis atque operibus, Berlin, 1845 ; *H. Swoboda*, P. N. F. operum reliquiae with Prolegomena, Vienna, 1889.

g. Ateius Praetextatus Philologus († c. 29 B.C.).
Cf. *Suet.* de gramm., 10 *T. S.*, § 211.

h. Noted philologists and grammarians of the Empire.
First Century.

1. *C. Iulius Hyginus*, pupil of Alexander Polyhistor, head of the Palatine library under Augustus. Cf. *Suet.* de gramm. et rhet. 20. Not to be confounded with the so-called Hyginus, author of the Genealogy, Astronomy and Fables.

Chief works (all lost) : Commentary to the Propempticon Pollionis of Helvius Cinna ; Commen-

tary to *Virgil* in at least 5 bks. (Cf. *Ribbeck* Proleg. Vergil. p. 117); *De vita rebusque inlustrium virorum; Exempla* (*Gell.* X 18, 7); *De familiis Troianis; Urbes Italicae* (*Serv.* ad Aen. VII 678); de proprietatibus deorum; de dis Penatibus.

2. *Fenestella* († 19 A.D.). 'diligentissimus scriptor,' Lactantius. *Annales* in at least 22 bks. A repository of information for later writers.

T. S. § 259; *L. Merklin*, De Fenestella historico et poeta, 1844.

3. M. VERRIUS FLACCUS (floruit 10 B.C.).

   α. *De verborum significatu.* Second half preserved in a mutilated *epitome* of *Festus*, who in turn was epitomized by *Paulus*. Inexhaustible fountain of information on Roman antiquities and archaic Latin.

   β. *Fasti*, partly preserved (C. I. L. I, 295). Used by Ovid.

Cf. *H. Winther*, De fastis V. F. ab Ovidio adhibitis, Berlin, 1885; *Hübner*, Grundr. der lat. Lit., § 83; *H. Nettleship*, Lectures and Essays, pp. 201 ff.; *T. S.* § 261.

4. Q. ASCONIUS PEDIANUS c. 3–88.

   (1) Commentary to *Cicero's speeches* — one of the masterpieces of historical exegesis in antiquity. Written betw. 54–57 A.D. Extant: pro Cornelio, in toga candida, in Pisonem, pro Scauro, pro Milone (with a highly valuable introduction).

Cf. *Madvig*, de Q. A. P. in Cic. oratt. commentariis, Kopenhagen, 1828; *C. Lichtenfeld*, De Q. A. P. fontibus ac fide (Bresl. Abh. II, 4 pp. 88).

   (2) Liber *contra obtrectatores Vergilii* (Lost).

Cf. *Donat.* Vita Verg. p. 66, 2 R.

   (3) Vita Sallustii — Doubtful, cited by *Ps. Acro* to Hor. Sat. I, 2, 41.

5. C. PLINIUS SECUNDUS, the Elder, 23–79.

(1) Libri *dubii sermonis* (*Plin.* Epist. III 5, 1).
(2) De grammatica (*Plin.* N. H. praef. 28).

Cf. *I. W. Beck*, Studia Gelliana et Pliniana, Lpz. 1892; *O. Froehde*, Valerii Probi de nomine libellum Plinii Secundi doctrinam continere demonstratur, Lpz. 1892.

6. M. VALERIUS PROBUS Berytius (flor. 80 A.D.).
The greatest Roman philologist. 'Nec Probum timeto' (Mart. III 2, 12).

(1) *Editions with critical signs* (cf. *Sueton.* Reliq., p.138 R.).
  α. *Virgil*
  Suringar, II, 8 ff.; *Kübler*, De P. comment. Verg., Berl. 1881.
  β. *Terence, Lucretius, Horace, Persius.*

(2) De notis singularibus.

Cf. *I. Steub*, De Probis grammaticis, Jena, 1871; *T. S.*, § 300 f.

7. FABIUS QUINTILIANUS of Calagurris in Spain, c. 35–95.
Literary criticism, esp. in bk. X of the Institutio Oratoria. Pupil of *Remmius Palaemon* (*T. S.*, § 282) and teacher of *Pliny* the Younger and *Cornelius Tacitus*. Cf. *Gudeman*, Tacitus' Dialogus, Proleg. p. XXVIII. LXII. LXXII.

Cf. *Peterson*, Quint. Bk. X Introd. pp. XXII–XXXIX.

8. C. SUETONIUS TRANQUILLUS, 75–160.

Cf. *Suidas* s. v. Τράγκυλλος; *Reifferscheid*, Suetoni Reliquiae praeter Caesares, Lpz. 1860 (Quaest. Suetonianae, pp. 363-538).

(1) *De viris illustribus*: de poetis, (Terence, Horace, Lucan, Persius — extant), de oratoribus, de historicis, de philosophis, and de grammaticis et rhetoribus (partially preserved).

(2) Περὶ τῶν ἐν τοῖς βιβλίοις σημείων, βιβλίον α΄ (Suidas) = de notis (cf. above).

(3) *Pratum* (de anno Romanorum, *Reiff.*, pp. 149–92; de naturis rerum, pp. 193–265; de genere vestium, pp. 266–72); περὶ δυσφήμων λέξεων ἤτοι βλασφημιῶν

καὶ πόθεν ἑκάστη (cf. *Etym. Magnum.* s. v. Ἀρχολί-
παρος and *Eust.* ad Iliad. II 234, VIII 488). *Verborum differentiae*, pp. 274–96.

(4) *Ludicra historia* (περὶ τῶν παρ' Ἕλλησι παιδιῶν), pp. 322–45.

(5) De lusibus puerorum. Part of 4 (?).

(6) De institutione officiorum.

(7) Περὶ τῆς Κικέρωνος πολιτείας ; ἀντιλέγει δὲ τῷ Διδύμῳ (see above, p. 20).

Second Century.

Aemilius Asper (*T. S.*, § 482, 3), Flavius Caper (*T. S.*, § 343, 3; *G. Keil*, De F. C. grammatico, in Diss. Hall. X, 243–306), Q. Terentius Scaurus (*T. S.*, § 352, 1), Arruntius Celsus (*T. S.*, § 357, 3), Iulius Romanus (*T. S.*, § 379, 1 ; *C. Froehde*, De I. R. Charisii auctore Leipz. 1892), *A. Gellius*, Noctes Atticae (*T. S.*, § 365 ; *Th. Vogel* De A. G. vita, studiis, scriptis 1860; *L. Ruske* De A. G. Noct. Att. fontibus 1883).

Third Century.

Censorinus, de die natali (*T. S.*, § 379).

Fourth Century.

1. *Nonius Marcellus*, Compendiosa Doctrina (*T. S.*, 404a; *L. Müller*, Adversaria to his edition).
2. Charisius and Diomedes (*T. S.*, § 419; *L. Jeep*, Zur Gesch. von. d. Redetheilen bei den Alten, Lpz. 1893).
3. Marius Victorinus (*T. S.*, § 408, 1).
4. *Aelius Donatus* (floruit c. 350).
   (1) *Grammatica.*
   (2) *Commentary to Terence.*
   (3) *Commentary to Virgil.*

Cf. *Gräfenhan*, IV, 107 ff. ; *Suringar*, I, 78–86 II 31–59 ; *T. S.*, § 409, 3 f.

5. Maurus *Servius* Honoratus.
   Commentary to *Virgil.*

Cf. *Suringar*, II, 59-92; *T. S.*, § 431; *G. Lämmerhirt*, De priscis scriptt. locis a S. allatis, in Comm. Philol. Ienens. IV, 311-406.

6. *Hieronymus*, 331-420.

Translation of the χρονικοὶ κανόνες of *Eusebius* with additions : "usque ad Troiae captivitatem pura graeca translatio est ... usque ad XX. Constantini annum nunc addita nunc mixta sunt plurima quae de Tranquillo (viz. *Sueton.* de viris illustribus) et ceteris inlustribus in historicis curiosissime excerpsi." On these sources, cf.

Mommsen, Abhandl. der sächsischen Gesell. d. Wiss. I (1850), 669 ff.

Fifth Century.

1. *Macrobius*, Saturnalia. (*T. S.*, § 444; *G. Wissowa*, De M. Saturn. fontibus, Breslau, 1888.)

2. *Priscian of Caesarea.*

Institutiones grammaticae, 18 bks. The most important and exhaustive contribution to Latin Grammar made by the Romans. An inexhaustible fountain of information for the grammatical theories of earlier writers, especially Greek, now lost. The standard work on the subject throughout the Middle Ages. About 1000 MSS. known.

Cf. *T. S.*, § 481, and Encyclop. Britan. s. v.

Sixth Century.

1. *Cassiodorus* Senator, 480-575.

Efforts to preserve classical literature. Copying of MSS. by his Benedictine monks.

2. Isidorus, c. 570-636.

Etymologiarum (Originum) libri XX (*T. S.*, § 496).

List of Extant Latin Scholia.

1. VERGILIUS:
   Scholia Bernensia to the Bucolics and Georgics. Introductory note to the latter: Haec omnia de [tribus] commentariis Romanorum congregavi *i.e.* Titi *Galli* et *Gaudentii* et maxime Iunilii Flagrii (= Iunius *Philargyrius*, part of whose commentary to the Eclogues is still extant).
   Scholia *Veronensia* to Aeneid (fragm.).
   Ps. Probus, see Probus.
   Donatus, Servius, see above.
   > Cf. *Suringar* II, 8–109. *Ribbeck*, Proleg. crit. ad Verg. c. 9.

2. HORATIUS:
   Porphyrio (largely indebted to Acro). *Ps. Acro* (chiefly based on Porphyrio. These scholia are handed down anonymously in the older MSS.); *Cruquianus commentator*, a congeries of scholia collected by Iac. Cruquius from his MSS., esp. the Blandinii.
   > Cf. *Suringar* III, 8–86; *H. Usener*, de scholiis Horat., Bern, 1863.

3. TERENTIUS:
   Donatus (made up of the original commentary of *Donatus* and of *Euanthius*. The scholia to the *Heaut.* are lacking); *Eugraphius*.
   > Cf. *Suringar* I, 78 ff.; *H. Usener*, Rhein. Mus. XXIII, 493 ff.; *H. Gerstenberg*, De Eugraphio T. interprete, Jena, 1886; *Sabbadini, R.*, Estr. dagli studi ital. di fil. class. II, pp. 1–132.

4. LUCANUS:
   Commenta (cod. Bern. 370), Adscriptiones (in a number of MSS.).

5. PERSIUS:
   Cornuti (?) commentum. c. 8th cent. Cf. *T. S.*, § 302, 6.

6. IUVENALIS:
   (*a*) In codd. *Pithoeanus* and *Sangallensis* (IX. cent). To

the same class belong the scholia (up to Sat. VIII 193), published by *Valla* under the name of Probus.
(b) *Cornuti* (?) expositio in MSS. of XV. cent.
   Cf. *T. S.*, 331, 7.
7. GERMANICUS, poetic paraphrase of *Aratus*.
   Cf. *Breysig*, Praef. to his edition and *Maass*, Proleg. to Aratus.
8. STATIUS' THEBAIS :
   Ad VI 264 : de his rebus . . . ex libris ineffabilis doctrinae Persei praeceptoris (Cornutus ?) seorsum libellum composui [Lactantius Placidus].

III. THE MIDDLE AGES.

1. THE BYZANTIAN PERIOD.

   K. Krumbacher, Grundriss der byzantinischen Literatur (I. Müller's Handbuch der class. Alterthumswissenschaft, vol. IX, 1), Characteristic of the period, pp. 214-17 ; *Wilamowitz*, Eur. Heracles, I, 193-219.

   a. *Hesychios* of Alexandria.
      Lexicon (Γλῶσσαι). Based upon the Περιεργοπένητες of Diogenianos.
      Cf. *Reitzenstein*, Rhein. Mus. XLIII, 443-460.
   b. *Hesychios Illustris* of Miletus (6. cent.)
      Ὀνοματόλογος ἢ πίναξ τῶν ἐν παιδείᾳ ὀνομαστῶν. Only preserved in excerpts. (Chief sources : Aelius Dionysius' Μουσικὴ ἱστορία, and Herennios Philon.)
      Cf. *Kr.*, pp. 110 ff.
   c. PHOTIOS, c. 820-c. 891.
      (1) Βιβλιοθήκη or Μυριόβιβλον (written before 857). Contains the excerpts and criticisms of 280 books read by the author while ambassador to Assyria.
      (2) Λέξεων συναγωγή (based on Harpocration, Diogenianos, Ἀττικῶν ὀνομάτων λόγοι of Aelius Dionysius, Pausanias' Λεξικὸν κατὰ στοιχεῖον, Platonic

lexicon of Timaeus, and Boethos, Homeric lexica of Apion, Heliodorus and Apollonius).
Cf. *Kr.*, pp. 223-33 ; *Fabricius*, Bibl. Gr. X, 678-775 XI, 1-37 ; *Hergenröther*, Photios, 3 vols., 1869.

d. Constantinos Porphyrogennetos, emperor (912-59, resp. 945). *Encyclopaedia of History*, arranged according to subject-matter (*e.g.* Περὶ Πρεσβειῶν, περὶ ἐπιβουλῶν κατὰ βασιλέων γεγονυιῶν, περὶ στρατηγημάτων, περὶ δημηγοριῶν), with the original chapters of earlier historians bearing upon the respective subjects. Cf. *Kr.*, pp. 59-69.

e. Suidas.
Lexicon (terminus post quem 976 A.D.). First cited by Eustathius. A colossal monument of erudition, notwithstanding many instances of gross carelessness. The sources of Suidas have as yet been determined with only partial accuracy, but he seems to have derived, though generally only at second-hand, the bulk of his material from the following :

α. *Lexica:* Harpocration, Aelius Dionysius, Pausanias, Helladios, Eudemos, Γλῶσσαι to Herodotus, and above all, *Hesychios* (cf. Suidas s. v. 'οὗ ἐπιτομή ἐστι τοῦτο τὸ βιβλίον'), Lexica to Euripides, Menander, Callimachus.

β. *Scholia and Commentaries to: Aristophanes* (in a more complete form than the extant scholia), Sophocles (Oed. Col., Oed. Tyr., Aiax), *Homer* (similar to those of the Venetus B), Thucydides, Philoponus and Alexander of Aphrodosias to Aristotle.

γ. *Histories:* Herodotus, Thucydides, Xenophon's Anabasis, Polybius, Josephus, Arrian, Aelian (probably from Constantinos' Encyclopaedia), Lucian.

δ. *Literary and Biographical material: Hesychios* (see

above), *Athenaeus* (bks. I and II in their unepitomized form). Whether the work of *Philon of Byblos* (see above) was known to Suidas at first-hand is very doubtful. *Strabo* is completely ignored.

Cf. *Fabricius*, Bibliotheca Graeca, VI, 389-595; *G. Bernhardy*, Suidae Lexicon, I, Prolegomena, pp. 25-95; *Kr.*, pp. 261-67; *R. Roellig*, Quae ratio inter Photii et Suidae lexica intercedat, in Diss. Hall. (1887) pp. 1-66.

f. Johannes Tzetzes, c. 1110-c. 1185.

(1) Βίβλος ἱστοριῶν (Chiliades), in 12,674 political verses.

Cf. *Chr. Harder*, De I. T. historiarum fontibus quaestiones, Kiel, 1886.

(2) *Allegories to the Iliad and Odyssey*, 10,000 verses. Ὁ Ὅμηρος ὁ πάνσοφος, ἡ θάλασσα τῶν λόγων. Homeric mythology interpreted allegorically and after the manner of Euhemerus.

(3) Commentary to the Iliad.

(4) Carmina Iliaca (Antehomerica, Homerica, Posthomerica).

(5) Scholia to Hesiod's Works and Days, and the Shield of Heracles (written before 1138).

(6) Scholia to Aristophanes' Plutos, Clouds, Frogs, and Arguments to the Knights and Birds.

Cf. *Ritschl (Keil)*, Opusc. I, 1-172. 197-237.

(7) Scholia to *Lycophron's Alexandra*.
Invaluable as the only extant key to the understanding of this enigmatical poem.

(8) Scholia to the Halieutica of *Oppian*, and the Theriaca and Alexipharmaca of *Nicandros*.

(9) Epitome of the Rhetoric of *Hermogenes*.

(10) Περὶ τῶν ἐν τοῖς στίχοις μέτρων ἁπάντων, στίχοι περὶ διαφορᾶς ποιητῶν. ἴαμβοι τεχνικοί περὶ κωμῳδίας, περὶ τραγικῆς ποιήσεως. .

Cf. *Kr.*, pp. 235-47.

g. *Eustathios*, Archbishop of Thessalonice (floruit 1175).
(1) *Commentary to the Iliad and Odyssey.*
Invaluable repository of ancient learning.

Principal sources: Homeric scholia, Athenaeus, Strabo, Stephanus of Byzantium, *Aristophanes* of Byzantium, Heraclides of Miletos, and two works by *Suetonius* (written in Greek); Aelios Dionysius, Pausanias, and rhetorical lexica, Suidas and the Etymologicum Magnum.

(2) Paraphrase and scholia to *Dionysius Periegetes.*
(3) Commentary to *Pindar* (only a valuable preface preserved).

Cf. *Kr.*, pp. 242-47; *Fabricius*, l. c., I, 457-501.

h. Maximus Planudes, 1260-1310.
(1) Περὶ γραμματικῆς, περὶ συντάξεως.
(2) Scholia to Theocritos and Hermogenes.
(3) Συναγωγὴ ἐκλεγεῖσα ἀπὸ διαφόρων βιβλίων, containing excerpts, e.g., from Plato, Aristotle, Strabo, Pausanias, Dio Cassius.
(4) *Anthologia Planudea.*
The *Anthologia Palatina* was not discovered till 1606 by Salmasius. Grotius' celebrated translation is based upon the Planudean collection.
(5) *Translations from Latin into Greek.*
α. Caesar, De bello Gallico.
β. Cicero, Somnium Scipionis.
γ. Disticha Catonis.
δ. Ovid, Metamorphoses.
ε. *Ovid, Heroides.* On the basis of a very valuable MS. now lost.

Cf. *A. G.*, in Calvary's Berl. Stud. VIII 3, pp. 90 (1888); *A. Palmer*, Ovid's Heroides, Oxford, 1894.

ζ. *Boethius*, De consolatione philosophiae (his masterpiece).

Cf. *M. Treu*, Comment. to Planudis Epistulae, Breslau, 1890;
A. G. in Proc. Am. Philol. Assoc. XX, 6 ff.; *Kr.*, pp. 248 f.

i. *Manuel Moschopulos* (pupil of Planudes).

  a. Ἐρωτήματα γραμματικά. Of great pedagogical influence toward the spread of Greek studies in the Renaissance. The famous grammar of *Melanchthon* is essentially a reproduction of the Ἐρωτήματα.

  Cf. *L. Voltz*, Jahrb. f. Phil., CXXXIX (1889), 579 ff.

  β. *Scholia* to the Iliad, bks. I and II. Hesiod, Pindar's Olymp. Odes, Euripides, Theocritos.

  Cf. *K. Hartfelder*, Philipp Melanchthon, Berl. 1889, pp. 225; *M. Treu*, l. c., pp. 208-12; *Kr.*, pp. 251 f.

k. *Thomas Magister* (contemporary of *i.*).

  (1) Ἐκλογὴ ὀνομάτων καὶ ῥημάτων Ἀττικῶν.

  (2) Scholia to Aesch., Soph., Eurip., to three comedies of Aristophanes.

  Cf. *Fr. Ritschl*, Thomae Magistri ecloga, Halle, 1832, with exhaustive Prolegomena; *Kr.*, pp. 253 f.

l. *Demetrius Triklinios* (beginning of 14. cent.).

  The foremost text critic among Byzantian philologians. Notable contributions to Greek versification.

  (1) Scholia to *Pindar;* author of two metrical dissertations, and of one of the extant paraphrases to Pindar (*Lehrs*, Pindarscholien, p. 78).

  (2) Text edition, with scholia, of *Sophocles.*

  (3) Scholia to five plays of *Aeschylos* (except Choephoroe and Supplices). Preserved in Triklinios' own handwriting.

  (4) Scholia to Hesiod, Aristophanes and Theocritos.

  Cf. *Wilamowitz*, Eur. Heracl. I, 194 f.; Hermes XXV, 161-70; *Kr.*, pp. 256 ff.

2. THE MIDDLE AGES IN W. EUROPE.

  Copying of MSS. in monasteries.

Cf. *A. H. L. Heeren*, Gesch. des Stud. der class. Literat. seit d. Wiederaufleben d. Wissensch., vol. I, Introduct., pp. 1-308 ; *F. Haase*, De medii aevi studiis philologis 1856; *F. A. West*, Alcuin and the schools of the West, 1890 ; *W. Wattenbach*, Schriftwesen im Mittelalter, 1875^2, Anleit. z. griech. Palaeographie, 1877^2, Anleit. z. lat. Palaeog. 1886^4 ; *Th. Birt*, Das antike Buchwesen, Berlin, 1882 ; *A. Ebert*, Allgem. Gesch. der Liter. des Mittelalters, 3 vols., 1887^2; *Bernhardy*, I^4, 716 ff.; *E. Hübner*, Encyclop., pp. 45-64 ; *M. Manitius*, Rhein. Mus. Suppl. XLVII, pp. 152 (catalogue of MSS. in cloister libraries); *Blass*, Palaeogr.^{2} pp. 299-355. Of mediaeval scholars who possessed a knowledge of *Greek*, the following may be mentioned : Bede, Ioh. Scotus Erigena, Alcuin, Abelard, Roger Bacon, Hrabanus Maurus.

LIST OF SOME OF THE OLDEST CLASSICAL MSS.

1. *Greek.*
   a. Fragments of Euripides' Antiope and Plato's Phaedo, 250 B.C. (Flinders Petrie Papyri, ed. Mahaffy, Dublin Acad. 1890.) The oldest specimens of a classical text known.
   b. A few lines of the *XI. Iliad* (ante-Aristarchean and non-Zenodotean), 240 B.C.
   Most of the following dates are only conjectural.
   c. Louvre fragments of *Euripides*, 2. cent. B.C.
   d. Alcman, 2.-1. cent. B.C.
   e. Iliad fragments (Banks, Harris), 2. cent. B.C.
   f. Papyri from *Herculaneum*, 79 A.D. (Epicurus, Philodemos.)
   g. Aristotle, Ἀθηναίων Πολιτεία, } 1.-2. cent. A.D.
   h. Herodas, Mimiambi.
   i. Four speeches of *Hypereides*, 150 A.D.
   k. Berlin fragm. of the *Melanippe* of *Euripides*, 3.-4. cent.
   l. Papyrus fragm. of *Isocrates*, 4. cent.
   m. Cod. Ambrosianus of the *Iliad.*
   n. Cod. Vaticanus of *Cassius Dio.* } 5.-6. cent.
   o. Euripides' *Phaeton* and *Menander*, frag.
   p. Fragm. of *Arist. Birds.*

2. *Latin*.
  a. Fragm. of Seneca, 1. cent.
  b. Seven oldest MSS. of *Virgil*, 3.–5. cent.
  c. Fragm. of *Sallust's* Historiae, 3.–4. cent.
  d. Codex Bembinus of *Terence*, 4.–5. cent.
  e. Codex Sessorianus of *Pliny*, N. H. 23–25, 5. cent.
  f. Codex Puteaneus of Livy, 6.–7. cent.
  g. *Palimpsesti.*
    α. Juvenal and Persius, frag. in cod. Vatic., 3.–4. cent.
    β. Codex Veronensis and cod. Vaticanus of *Livy*.
    γ. *Lucan* (Vienna, Naples, Rome), 4. cent.
    δ. *Cicero's De republica*, 4.–5. cent.
    ε. Cicero in Verrem, fragm. in cod. Vatic., 5. cent.
    ζ. *Plautus* (cod. Ambrosianus), 5.–6. cent.
    η. Gellius and Seneca, fragm., 5.–6. cent.
    θ. *Fronto*, fragm., 4.–6. cent.
    ι. Livy, fragm. (Vienna), 5. cent.

IV. THE REVIVAL OF LEARNING IN ITALY.

Cf. *G. Voigt*, Die Wiederbelebung des class. Alterthums, 2 vols., Berlin, 1894[3]; *J. A. Symonds*, Renaissance in Italy (vol. II. The Revival of Learning), 1877; *J. Burkhardt*, Die Cultur der Renaissance in Italien, 1885[5]; *D. Comparetti*, Virgilio nel medio evo, 2 vols., Livorno, 1872; *Alfred von Reumont*, Lorenzo de' Medici, il Magnifico, 2 vols. (1874), pp. 606. 604, esp. I, 517–606 II, 1–149; *F. A. Eckstein*, Nomenclator philologorum, Lpz. 1871, pp. 656; *W. Pökel*, Philolog. Schriftstellerlexicon, Lpz. 1882.

(A) GREEK IMMIGRANTS.

Cf. *H. Hodius*, De Graecis illustr. linguae Graecae litterarumque humaniorum instauratoribus, 1742; *Bernhardy*, 1[4], 730 ff.

(1) *Manuel Chrysoloras*, 1350–1415.

In Florence in 1396, thereafter in Pavia, Venice, Rome. Died in Germany. Niccoli, Bruni, Marsuppini, Traversari were among his pupils.

  a. Ἐρωτήματα τῆς Ἑλληνικῆς.

b. Verbatim translation of *Plato's* Republic.

Cf. *Voigt*, I, 225-35; *Symonds*, pp. 108 ff.

(2) *Georgios Gemisthios Plethon*, 1355-1452.
Famous Platonist.

Voigt, II, 119-22 ; *Symonds*, pp. 198-210; *F. Schultze*, G. G. P., Iena, 1874, pp. 320.

(3) *Bessarion*, 1403-72.
Pupil of Plethon. Famous library of 800 MSS bequeathed to Venice (the foundation of the St. Marcus Library). Translator of *Arist. Metaphysics*, *Xenophon's* Memorabilia.

Cf. *Voigt*, II, 124-33; *Symonds*, pp. 247 ff.; *H. Vast*, Le Cardinal Bessarion, Paris, 1879.

(4) *Theodorus Gaza*, c. 1400-c. 1478.
   a. Γραμματικὴ εἰσαγωγή.
   b. Celebrated translations of : *Aristotle*, Theophrastus de plantis, Aelian, Dionysius De compositione verborum. Cicero de sen. and de amicit. into Greek.

Cf. *Hody*, pp. 55-101 ; *Voigt*, II, 145 ff.; *L. Stein*, Archiv f. Gesch. der Philosophie, II 3, pp. 426-58.

(5) *Demetrius Chalcondylas*, 1428-1510.
   a. Edition of *Homer* (ed. pr. 1488), *Isocrates, Suidas*.
   b. Ἐρωτήματα.

Cf. *Hody*, pp. 211-26 ; *Voigt*, I, 442.

(6) *Constantinos Lascaris* († after 1500).
   a. Ἐρωτήματα (Milan, 1476. First Greek book ever printed).

Cf. *Voigt*, I, 371 II, 148 ; *A. F. Villemain*, Lascaris, Paris, 1825 (Engl. transl. 1875, London).

(B) Italian Humanists.

(1) *Francesco Petrarca*, 1304-74.
Discoverer of Cicero's Letters.

Cf. *Voigt*, I, 12–159; *Symonds*, pp. 69–87; *Th. Campbell*, Life and Times of Petrarca, 1845²; *L. Geiger*, Petrarka, 1874, pp. 267; *G. Körting*, P. Leben u. Werke, Lpz. 1878; and esp. *P. de Nolhac*, Pétrarque et l'humanisme, Paris, 1892, pp. 439.

(2) *Giovanni Boccaccio*, 1313–75.
  a. *Genealogia* deorum gentilium.
  b. De casibus illustrium virorum.
  c. De claris mulieribus.
  d. De montibus, silvis, fontibus, lacubus, fluminibus.

Cf. *G. Körting*, B.'s Leben u. Werke, pp. 742, Lpz. 1880; *Voigt*, I, 165–86; *Symonds*, pp. 87–97. 133.

(3) *Colutius Salutatus* (Coluccio de Piero de Salutati), 1330–1406.

Cf. *Voigt*, I, 194–214 II 192. 486; *Symonds*, pp. 103 ff.

(4) *Leonardo Bruni* (Aretinus), 1369–1444.
  Celebrated translations of *Aristotle*, Demosthenes, Plutarch.

Cf. *Voigt*, I, 309 ff. II, 165 ff.

(5) *Francesco Poggio Bracciolini*, 1380–1459.
  Discoverer of MSS of *Cicero* (seven orations), Asconius Pedianus' Commentary to Cicero's speeches, *Plautus* (XII new comedies), a complete *Quintilian*, Ammianus Marcellinus, Aratea, Silius, Manilius, Columella, Frontinus, *Nonius*, Probus, *Petronius*, parts of *Lucretius*, Valerius Flaccus, Priscian, Vitruvius, Statius' Silvae [*Tacitus*, Dial., Germ., *Suet.* de gramm.].

Cf. *Voigt*, I, 237–62 II, 7.75. 254 ff. 329–342; *Symonds*, pp. 134 ff. 230–46; *Henzen* in C. I. L. VI 1 (on P.'s contributions to epigraphy); *Ch. Nisard*, Les gladiateurs de la République des lettres aux XVe, XVIe, XVIIe siècles, 1860, pp. 117–194.

(6) *Victorinus da Feltre*, 1379–1447.
  Celebrated pedagogue.

Cf. *Voigt*, I, 537 ff.; *Symonds*, pp. 289–97.

(7) *Kyriacus of Ancona*, 1391–c. 1450.
"I go to awake the dead." Famous collector of inscriptions in Greece and Italy. "Maiorem quam ipsi libri fidem et notitiam praebere videbantur" (sc. inscriptiones).

Cf. *Voigt*, I, 271–88; C. I. L. III, p. xxii, 129 ff.; *E. Hübner*, Röm. Epigraphik (= I. Müller's Handbuch, vol. I²); *Symonds*, pp. 155 ff.; *B. de Rossi*, Inscript. Christ. II, 356–387.

(8) *Giovanni Aurispa*, c. 1370–1459.
Famous collector of Greek MSS. Reached *Venice* in 1423, with 238 *vols.*, containing mostly classical authors purchased in Constantinople. Among his priceless treasures were the celebrated codex Laurentianus (seven plays of *Soph.*, six of *Aesch.*, *Apollonius'* Argonautica), of the X. cent., now in Florence, *Iliad* (Venet. A), *Athenaeus*, the entire *Demosthenes*, and *Plato*, *Xenophon*, *Diodorus*, *Strabo*, *Arrian*, *Lucian*, *Dio Cassius*.

Cf. *Voigt*, I, 262 ff. 560 ff. II, 348.

(9) *Francesco Filelfo* (Philelphus), 1398–1481.
Itinerant professor; collector of MSS. Translator of Homer.

Cf. *Voigt*, I. 351–69; *Symonds*, pp. 267–89; *G. Favre*, Mélanges d'histoire littéraire, vol. I, pp. 9–146, Genève, 1856; *Nisard*, pp. 1–115.

(10) *Laurentius Valla* (Lorenzo della Valle), 1407–57.
   a. *Elegantiae Latini sermonis*, 1444. 59. edit. in 1536. Still useful.
   b. Translations: Herodotus, Thucydides, Homer.
   c. Edition of *Quintilian*, printed 1494.

Cf. *J. Vahlen*, Lorenzo Valla, Vienna, 1870; *Voigt*, I, 464–80 II, 181 f.; *Symonds*, pp. 258–65; *Nisard*, pp. 195–304; *Mancini*, G., L. V. pp. 339, Florence, 1891.

(11) *Marsilius Ficinus* (Marsiglio Ficino), 1433–99.
Famous translation of *Plato*.

Cf. *Creuzer,* Opusc. II 5, pp. 10–21; *Voigt,* II, 123. 326; *Symonds,* pp. 324 ff.

(12) *Angelus Politianus* (Angiolo de' Ambrosini of Monte Puliciano), 1454–98.
Praefationes to Homer, Quintilian, Statius' Silvae, Suetonius, Praelectio in Persium. Translation of *Callimachus,* Herodianos and Epictetus.

Cf. *Heeren,* l. c., II, 247–69; *Voigt,* I, 371 II, 199; *Symonds,* pp. 345–55.

(13) Petrus VICTORIUS (Pietro Vettori), 1499–1584.
The greatest philologist and critic of the Italian Renaissance.
  a. Edition of *Cicero,* with commentary.
  b. Edition of *Sophocles,* with comment. and the scholia, 1547. The *Electra* published for the first time in 1545. *Aeschylus,* 1557.
  c. Edition, commentary and translation of *Aristotle,* (Ethics, Rhetoric, Poetics, de partibus animalium, Politics).
  d. Xenophon's Memorabilia.
  e. Terence ; Sallust ; Varro, de re rustica.
  f. Demetrius [Phalereus] de elocutione, Dionysius, Isaeus, Dinarchus, Hipparchus in Arati et Eudoxi Phaenomena, Clemens Alexandrinus, Porphyrius de abstinentia.
  g. *Variae lectiones,* 38 bks.

Cf. *Bandini,* Petri Victorii vita, Florence, 1758 ; *Fr. Creuzer,* l. c., pp. 21–36 ; *H. Kämmel,* Jahn's Jahrb. XCV, 545 ff.; XCVI, 325 ff. 421 ff.

A LIST OF THE MORE IMPORTANT EDITIONES PRINCIPES OF CLASSICAL AUTHORS.

Cf. *Chr. Saxe,* Onomasticon, 2 vols., 1775–90; *I. I. Brunet,* Manuel de Libraire, etc., 8 vols., 1880 ; *F. A. Schweiger,* Handbuch d. class. Bibliographie, 2 vols., 1830–34; *S. F. G. Hoffmann,*

Lex. Bibliographicum, 3 vols. (only Greek authors), 1832; *L. Hain*, Reportorium bibliographicum, ab arte typographia inventa usque ad a MD, 4 vols., Paris and Stuttgart, 1838; *Renouard*, Annales de l'imprimerie des Aldes, Paris, 1834³; *Schück*, Aldus Manutius u. seine Zeitgenossen, Berlin, 1862; *A. F. Didot*, Alde Manuce, pp. LXVIII + 647, Paris, 1875.

1. *Greek.*

- 1481. Theocritos (Id. I–XVIII), together with Hesiod, Works and Days.
- 1488. Homer (ed. Chalcondylas). Valla's Latin. transl. of the Iliad was printed as early as 1474.
- 1495. Hesiod, Opera omnia (Aldus).
- 1495–98. Aristotle (Aldus).
- 1496. Euripides' Med., Hypp., Alc., Androm. (I. Lascaris), Apollonius (Lascaris), Lucian (in Florence).
- 1498. Aristophanes (excl. Lys. and Thesm.); Opera omnia. Basle, 1532.
- 1499. Aratus (in: Astronomi vett. ap. Aldum).
- 1500. Callimachus' Hymns (Lascaris).
- 1502. Herodotus, Thucydides, Sophocles (Aldi).
- 1503. Euripides' Opera (excl. Electra, edit. by Victorius, 1545, from Cod. Laurent. 32, 2).
- 1513. Plato, Oratt. Att. [Hyperides, papyrus discovered 1847]. Pindar (together with Callim., Dionys., Perierg., Lycophron) (Aldus).
- 1514. Athenaeus (Aldus).
- 1516. Xenophon (excl. Agesil., Apologia, Πόροι, ap. Iunta), Opera omnia, 1525, ap. Aldum; Strabo (transl. printed in Rome, 1470), Pausanias.
- 1518. Aeschylus (Aldus).
- 1530. Polybius (ap. Vincent. Opsopocus, *i.e.* Koch). Latin transl. by Nic. Perrotto (bks. I–V), printed 1473.
- 1533. Diogenes Laertius (Froben, Basle).

1539. Diodorus (libb. 16–20). Latin transl. (libb.–I–V) by Poggio, 1472.
1544. Iosephus (Basle).
1548. Cassius Dio (R. Stephanus).
1551. Appian.
1572. Plutarch (H. Stephanus). Latin transl. by Campanus, 1471.

2. *Latin.*

1465. Cicero, de officiis. First printed edition of a classical author. Cf. art. 'Typography' in Encycl. Brit. Lactantius (Rome).
1469. Caesar, Virgil, Livy, Lucan, Apuleius, Gellius (Rome).
1470. Persius, Juvenal, Martial, Quintilian, Suetonius (Rome). Tacitus, Juvenal, Sallust, Horace (Venice). Terence (Strassburg).
1471. Ovid (Rome, Bonn), Nepos (Venice).
1472. Plautus (G. Merula), Catullus, Tibullus, Propertius, Statius (Venice).
1473. Lucretius (Brixiae).
1474. Valerius Flaccus (Bonn).
1475. Seneca (Prose Works), Sallust (*first* volume issued in *octavo*).
1484. Seneca (Tragedies) at Ferrara.
1485. Pliny the Younger (Venice).
1498. Cicero, Opera omnia.
1520. Vell. Paterculus (Beatus Rhenanus, Basle). Only one MS in existence.

V. FRANCE.

Cf. *E. Egger*, L'Hellénisme en France, 2 vols., 1869; *A. Lefranc*, Histoire du Collège de France, 1892.

(1) *Robert Etienne* (Stephanus), 1503–69.

Learned printer of classical authors, e.g. Horace,

Dionysius Hallic. Dio Cassius. *Thesaurus* linguae Latinae, 1531–6.

(2) HENRI ETIENNE, son of Robert, 1528–98.

Thesaurus graecae linguae, 5 vols., 1572; reëdited by Dindorf, 1865. Still the most complete lexicon of Greek published.

Cf. *Egger*, l.c., pp. 198 ff.; *M. Pattison*, Essays, I, 66–124; *L. Feugère*, Essai sur la vie et les ouvrages de H. E., Paris, 1853; *Pökel* (list of his numerous editions).

(3) *Adrien Turnèbe* (Turnebus), 1512–65.
Celebrated *critic*. Editor e.g. Aesch. *Soph.*, Arist. Ethics, Theophrastus, Philo., *Cicero de legg.* Commentaries to *Varro* de ling. Lat., and Horace, *Adversaria*, 30 bks. Cf. *Pökel* s. v.

(4) DENIS LAMBIN (DIONYSIUS LAMBINUS), 1520–72.
Famous commentator and critic of *Horace, Cicero, Lucretius, Plautus*, Nepos.

Cf. *Orelli*, Onomasticon Ciceronis, vol. I, Appendix, pp. 478–91.

(5) *Marcus Antonius Muretus*, 1526–85.
Renowned Latin stylist and critic.

Editions and commentaries to *Terence, Catullus, Tibullus, Propertius*, Seneca; *Cicero's Philippics. Variae lectiones.*

Cf. Opera omnia, ed. *D. Ruhnken*, 4 vols. 1789 (Life in Vol. IV, 518–82); *Frotscher*, 3 vols., 1834; *C. Dejob*, M. A. Muret, Paris, 1881 (iv, pp. 496); *M. Pattison*, Essays I, 124–132.

On *Scaliger*, see below.

(6) ISAAC CASAUBON (Casaubonus), 1559–1614.
Next to Scaliger the greatest πολυίστωρ of his time.
"Est doctissimus omnium qui hodie vivunt," Scaligerana.

a. De Satyrica Graeca poesi et Romanorum satira, 1605 (ed. Rambach, Halle, 1774).

b. Editions and commentaries:
  a. Theophrastus, Characters. 1592.

β. *Athenaeus*, 1598.   1840[8] (incorporated into Schweighäuser's edition).

γ. *Persius*, 1605.   1833[4].

δ. *Suetonius*, 1595.   1611[3] (cf. F. A. Wolf's edition).

ε. *Polybius*, 1609.   (Especially noteworthy for its introduction on *Greek Historiography*.)

ζ. Apuleius, Strabon, Polyaenos (ed. pr.) Histor. Aug. Script., Aristophanes.

η. Exegetical and critical contributions to Dionysius Halic., Pliny the Younger, Theocritos, Diogenes Laertius.

Cf. *Mark Pattison*, Isaac Casaubon, Oxford, 1892[2] (ed. Nettleship).

On *Salmasius*, see below.

(7) Charles du Fresne sieur *du Cange*, 1610–88.

  a. *Glossarium ad scriptores mediae et infimae Latinitatis*, 1678.

  b. *Glossarium ad scriptores mediae et infimae Graecitatis*, 1688.

  c. Edition of Byzantian Historians, 1680.

Cf. *Hardouin*, Essai sur la vie et les ouvrages de du Cange, Paris, 1849.

(8) *Bernard de Montfaucon*, 1655–1741.

Cf. *E. de Broglie*, La société de l'abbaye de Saint-Germain, etc., 1891, 2 vols.

  a. *Palaeographia Graeca*, 1708 f.

  b. L'antiquité expliquée et représentée en figures, 10 vols. fol. (1719), Suppl. 5 vols. fol. (1724). 1757[2].

VI. THE NETHERLANDS.

Cf. *L. Müller*, Gesch. der class. Philologie in den Niederlanden, Lpz. 1869 (pp. 249); *G. D. I. Schotel*, De Academie te Leiden in de 16ᵉ, 17ᵉ en 18º Eeuw, Haarlem, 1875, pp. 410.

DESIDERIUS ERASMUS of Rotterdam, 1465–1536.

Cf. *H. Durand de Laur*, Erasme, 2 vols. (pp. 694, 596), Paris, 1872; *R. B. Drummond*, E., his Life and Character, 2 vols.

(pp. 413, 380), London, 1873; *L. Feugère*, Erasme, Paris, 1874; *A. R. Pennington*, Life and Character of E., London, 1875; *Pökel*, l.c. p. 71 f.

1. FIRST PERIOD, 1530–75.
   (1) Adriaan de Jonghe (*Hadrianus Junius*), 1511–75.
   Plutarch, Symp., Martial, Nonius Marcellus, Animadversiones, 6 bks. — nomenclator octilinguis.
   (2) *Jacque de Crusque* (Cruquius), † 1584.
   Editor of *Horace* with scholia, 1578.
   (3) *Wilhelm Canter*, 1541–75.
   Editions of Aesch., Soph., Eur., Aristides, Stobaeus. Trans. of Lycophron's Alexandra (in Scaliger's edition).

2. SECOND PERIOD, 1575–1650.
   Foundation of the University of Leyden, 1575; Utrecht, 1636. Cf. *L. Müller*, p. 5 ff.
   (1) JUSTUS LIPSIUS, 1547–1606.
   1567 in Rome, 1572 Professor in Jena, 1576 in Löwen, 1579 in Leyden, 1592 in Löwen.
   a. TACITUS, 1574[1]. Epoch-making masterpiece.
   b. Velleius Paterculus, 1591. Cf. *Ruhnken*, Opusc. II, p. 541.
   c. Seneca Philosophus, 1605.
   d. Valerius Maximus.
   Cf. *A. de Reiffenberg*, De J. L. vita et scriptis commentarius, Brussels, 1823; *L. Müller*, pp. 24–29. 33–35.
   (2) JOSEPH JUSTUS SCALIGER, 1540–1609.
   Wyttenbach, Praef. ad Plut. Moralia 'Unus forte Joseph Scaliger, quem ex omnibus qui post renatas Literas fuerunt, omni Antiquitatis scientia consumatissimum fuisse constat, non multum ab hac perfectione abfuit.' "The most richly stored intellect which ever spent itself in aquiring knowledge" Pattison.

"Melius morbos quam remedia novimus" Scaliger.
Born in France. Called to Leyden in 1593.
a. Coniectanea to Varro, De L. L., 1565.
b. Catalecta Virgilii et aliorum poetarum veterum, 1572.
c. FESTUS, 1575.
d. Catullus, Tibullus, Propertius, 1577.
e. Manilius, 1579.
f. DE EMENDATIONE TEMPORUM, 1583.
g. THESAURUS TEMPORUM, 1606.
h. TWENTY-FOUR INDEXES TO GRUTER'S THESAURUS INSCRIP. LATIN., 1601.
i. De re nummaria, 1616; Opuscula, 1610; De arte critica, 1619.

Cf. *J. Bernays*, J. J. Scaliger, Berlin, 1855 (pp. 319); List of works, l. c. pp. 267-305; *L. Müller*, pp. 35. 222-7; *M. Pattison*, Essays, Vol. I, 196-244; *Ruhnkenius*, Elog. Hemsterhusii (Opusc. I, 269).

(3) *Gerhard Johannes Vossius,* 1577-1649.
    1615 in Leyden, 1622 in Amsterdam.
  a. Grammatica Latina (1607), *Aristarchus* (1635), de vitiis sermonis (1640), Etymologicum (1660).
  b. Ars rhetorum, de arte poetica (1647).
  c. DE HISTORICIS GRAECIS, 1634 (1833 ed. Westermann).
  d. De historicis Latinis, 1627.
  Cf. *L. Müller*, p. 39 f.; *Pökel*, s. v.

(4) *Daniel Heinsius,* 1581-1639.
    Editor of Hesiod, Theocritos, Terence, Virgil, Horace, *Ovid,* Seneca, *Silius.*
    Cf. *L. Müller,* p. 38 f.

(5) Claude de Saumaise (SALMASIUS), 1588-1653.
    Professor in Leyden, 1631. At the court of Christina of Sweden, 1650. Opponent of Milton. Discoverer of Kephalas' Anthologia, 1606.

"Non homini sed scientiae deest quod nescivit Salmasius."
— Balzac.

    a. Hist. Aug. Scriptt. 1620; Florus, 1609; Tertullian.
    b. *Plinianae exercitatt.* in Solinum, 1629.
    c. De lingua hellenistica, 1643.
    d. De usuris, de mutuo, de annis climactericis.
    e. De re militari Romanorum, 1657.
    Cf. *Saxe*, Onomast. IV, 188 ff.; *F. Creuzer*, l. c. pp. 65–75; *L. Müller*, p. 41.

(6) *Hugo Grotius*, 1583–1645.
    'Aliter pueri Terentium legunt, aliter Grotius.'
    a. Famous transl. of the *Anthol. Planudea*, 1645.
    b. *De iure belli et pacis*, 1625[1].
    c. Editions of: Mart. Capella, Lucan's Pharsalia, Silius Italicus.
    Cf. *Creuzer*, l. c. p. 80 ff.; *L. Müller*, p. 38; *H. de Vries*, H. G. 1827; *Pökel.* s. v.

3. THIRD PERIOD, 1650–1750.
    (1) Joh. Friedrich *Gronov*, 1611–1671.
    "Numquam interituram esse veram educationem donec Gronovii opera legentur." — Markland.

    Editor of: Sallust, both Senecas, the two Plinys, Tacitus, Gellius, Justinus, Plautus, Phaedrus, Statius, Martial.
    Cf. *L. Müller*, pp. 42–44.

    (2) Jacob *Gronov*, 1645–1716, son of (1).
    a. Editor of: Herodotus, Polybius, Cicero, Ammianus.
    b. *Thesaurus Antiquitatum Graecarum*, 13 vols., 1702.

    (3) *Nicolaus Heinsius* (son of Daniel H.), 1620–81.
    Editions and commentaries of: Virgil, Ovid, Valerius Flaccus, Silius, Claudianus, Prudentius, Petronius, Velleius, Curtius, Tacitus.
    Cf. *L. Müller*, pp. 51–54.

(4) Joh. Georg *Graevius*, 1623–1703.

Editor of : *Ciceronis* Opera omnia, Hesiod, Callimachus, Iustinus, Catullus, Tibullus, Propertius, Florus. *Thesaurus Antiquitatum Romanorum*, 12 vols., 1699..

Cf. *L. Müller*, pp. 44 f.

(5) *Ezechiel Spanheim*, 1629–1710.

Born in Geneva, died in London. Educated in Leyden.

a. Famous and still useful commentary to the *Hymns* of *Callimachus*, ed. Ernesti, 1761, in 2 vols.

b. Dissertatio *de usu et praestantia numismatum antiquorum*, 1664, 1706^8.

Cf. *D. Ruhnken*, Opusc. II, 596 f.

(6) *Peter Burmann* the elder, 1668–1741.

Editor of : Petronius, Velleius, Quintilian, Suetonius, Aristophanes, Phaedrus, Lucan, Valerius Flaccus.

Cf. *L. Müller*, pp. 45, f. 54–59; *Saxe*, Onomast. V, 466–77.

(7) Peter *Burmann* [Secundus], nephew of (6), 1714–78.

Editor of : Virgil, Propertius, Claudianus, *Poetae Minores, Anthologia Latina*.

Cf. *T. C. Harles*, Vitae Philologorum nostra aetate clarissimorum, vol. I, 93–167.

(8) Tiberius Hemsterhuis (HEMSTERHUSIUS), 1685–1766.

Prof. in Franeker 1717, in Leyden 1740. Resuscitator of Greek studies in Holland.

Editions of *Pollux* (1706), *Lucian* and *Aristoph. Plutos*.

Cf. *D. Ruhnken*, Elogium H., pp. 1–33, with notes by Bergman, pp. 303–336; *L. Müller*, pp. 74–82.

4. FOURTH PERIOD, 1750 to the present.
  (1) Ludwig Caspar *Valckenaer*, 1715–85.
    Prof. in Franeker, 1741; in Leyden, 1766.
    a. Editions of: Homer, Iliad with scholia, 1747.
    EURIPIDIS PHOENISSAE, 1755 (1824⁴, Lpz. 2 vols.).
    Euripidis Hippol. acced. DIATRIBE IN EUR. PERDIT.
    FABB. RELL. 1768 (1823, Lpz. 2 vols.).
    THEOCRITOS, *Bion and Moschus*, 1781. Poetae bucolici et didactici ed. ill. 1781.
    Callimachi fragmenta, ed. Luzac, 1799.
    b. DIATRIBE DE ARISTOBULO ed. Luzac, 1806.
    c. F. Ursinus, *Vergilius* collatione scriptt. Graec. illustr. ed. Valck., 1747.
      Cf. *Wyttenbach*, Vita Ruhnkenii, pp. 175-181; *L. Müller*, pp. 82 f.
  (2) David Ruhneken (RUHNKENIUS), 1723–98.
    Prof. at Leyden., born in Germany.
    a. *Timaei lexicon* vocum Platonicarum, 1754 (1833⁴).
    b. Oratio de doctore umbratico, Leyden, 1761.
    c. *Historia critica oratorum Graecorum*, 1768 (Lpz. 1841).
    d. (P. J. Schardam) De vita et scriptis *Longini*.
    e. Velleius, Homeric Hymns to Demeter and Dionysos.
    f. Dictata in Terentium, in Ovidii Heroidas, in Suetonium.
      Cf. *D. Wyttenbach*, Vita D. Ruhnkenii, pp. 67-300, ed. with notes by Bergman, pp. 353-494 (1824); *L. Müller*, pp. 84-8, 101-3.
  (3) *Daniel Wyttenbach*, 1746–1820.
    a. PLUTARCHI MORALIA (Text, *Animadversiones*, index, 14 vols.; Commentary unfinished), 1795–1820. Plato's Phaedo.
    b. Philomathia, 3 vols., 1817. Bibliotheca Critica, 1779–1809. *Vita Ruhnkenii*, 1790.
      Cf. *L. Müller*, pp. 91-6; *Mahne*, Vita D. Wyttenbachi, 1823.

(4) *Peter Hofman-Peerlkamp*, 1786–1865.
Editions of: Tacitus' Agricola; *Horace*, Odes (1834), Satires (1845) and Ars Poetica (1863); Virgil's Aeneid (1863); Propertius, 1865.

Cf. *L. Müller*, pp. 110 f.

(5) *C. Gabriel Cobet*, 1813–89.
Prof. in Leyden.
  a. Oratio de arte interpretandi, 1847.
  b. Diogenes Laertius, Paris, 1850; Lysias, 1863.
  c. Novae Lectiones, 2 vols. Variae Lectiones, 2 vols.

Cf. *J. J. Hartmann*, Biogr. Jahrbuch (Calvary), XII, 53 ff. (1889).

VII. ENGLAND.

Burney's Pleiad: Bentley, [Dawes], Markland, Taylor, [Toup, Tyrwhitt], Porson.

(1) RICHARD BENTLEY, 1662–1742.

"Nobis et ratio et res ipsa centum codd. potiores sunt."—To Hor. C. III, 27, 13.

1676 in Cambridge, 1689 in Oxford, 1694 in London, 1700 Master of Trinity College, Cambridge.
  a. Epistola ad Millium, 1691.
  b. DISSERTATION ON THE EPISTLES OF PHALARIS, etc., 1690 (ed. W. Wagner, 1874). Immortal masterpiece.
  c. HORACE, 1711. 1869 (ed. Zangemeister). Epoch-making masterpiece.
  d. Discovery of the *Digamma* in *Homer* (Collins on Freethinking, 1713, ed. of Milton, 1732).
  e. Terence (Famous introduction on *Latin Versification*), with Phaedrus, Publilius Syrus, 1726.
  f. Collection of the fragments of CALLIMACHUS, 1693.
  g. Manilius (1739); Emendations to Menander and Philemon (1710).

Cf. *J. H. Monk*, Life of R. B., 2 vols. 1833^2 (I, 428 II, 466); *F. A. Wolf*, Literar. Analecten I, 1–95 II, 493–9 (= Klein. Schrift. II, 1030–1089 ff.); *R. C. Jebb*, R. B. (Engl. Men of Letters), Lond. 1882 (pp. 224); *J. Mähly*, R. B., 1868 (pp. 179). *Bernays*, Philol. Mus. VIII, 1–24.

(2) *Jeremiah Markland*, 1693–1776.

Editor of *Euripides*, Maximus Tyrius, *Statius' Sylvae*. Remarks on the *Epistles of Cicero to Brutus*, 1745.

Cf. *Wolf*, Analecten, II, 370–91.

(3) *John Taylor*, 1703–66.

Editor of *Lysias*, 1739; Aeschines, 1769; several orations of Demosthenes.

Cf. *Wolf*, l. c. I, 500 ff.

(4) RICHARD PORSON, 1759–1808.

Next to Bentley, England's greatest text critic. Prof. in Cambridge, 1792; Librarian of the London Institution, 1805.

a. Aeschylus, 1795, 2 vols.

b. EURIP. HECUBA, 1797, with suppl. to the famous preface on *Greek versification* [Canon Porsonianus], 1808.

c. Eurip. Orest. 1798; Phoen. 1799; Medea, 1801.

d. Critical contributions to Homer, Herodotus, Xenophon, Aristoph., Pausanias, Suidas.

Cf. *J. S. Watson*, Life of R. P., 1861; *F. A. Wolf*, Anal. II, 284–9; *G. Hermann*, Opusc. VI, 92 ff. Tracts and Miscellaneous Criticism of R. P., edited by *Kidd*, 1815.

(5) *Peter Elmsley*, 1773–1825.

Editions of: Thucydides; *Eurip*. Alc., Androm., Elect., Med., Heracl., Bacch.; *Aristoph*., Acharn., with comment., 1809. Soph., O. T., O. C.

(6) William Martin *Leake*, 1777–1869.

Celebrated traveler and archaeologist.

OF CLASSICAL PHILOLOGY.   63

  a. Topography of Athens and the demi.
  b. Travels in Northern Greece, 1841, 4 vols.
  c. Travels in the Morea, 1830, 2 vols.
  Cf. *J. H. Marsden*, Memoir on the Life and Writings of W. M. L., London, 1864; *E. Curtius*, Alterthum u. Gegenwart II, 305–323.

(7) *Thomas Gaisford*, 1779–1855.
  Edition of: *Hephaestion, Procli* Chrestom., *Suidas*, 3 vols., Scriptt. lat. rei metricae, Paroemiogr. Graec., *Etymol. Magn. Stobaeus, Eusebius*, 6 vols.

(8) *George Grote*, 1794–1871.
  a. GREEK HISTORY, 12 vols., 1856.
  b. *Plato* and the other companions of Socrates, 1865.
  c. Aristotle (unfinished), 1871.
  Cf. *Harriett Grote*, G. G. 1873; Biogr. Jahrb. I, 31 ff.

(9) Hugh Andrew Johnstone *Munro*, 1819–85.
  a. LUCRETIUS (text, comment., transl.), 3 vols., 1873. 1886[4].
  b. Lucil. Aetna, text and comment., 1867.
  c. Horace, 1869.
  d. Criticisms and Elucidations of *Catullus*, 1878.
  Cf. *J. D. Duff*, Biogr. Jahrb. VII, 111 ff.

(10) *Benjamin Jowett*, 1817–1893.
  Translations of: The Dialogues of PLATO, 5 vols., 1892[3]; *Thucydides* with Commentary, 2 vols. 1881; *Politics* of Aristotle, 1885.

VIII. GERMANY.

  Chief work: *C. Bursian*, Geschichte der class. Philologie in Deutschland von den Anfängen bis zur Gegenwart, Munich, 1883 (pp. VIII+1271); *Hübner*, l. c. pp. 99–121.

(A) ANTE-WOLFIAN PERIOD.

  (1) Roclef Huysman (*Rudolphus Agricola*), 1442/3–85.
  Famous pedagogue. The first to introduce the systematic study of the classics into Germany. Trans-

lation of Ps. Plato's Axiochus, several treatises of Lucian. Commentary to Seneca Rhetor.

Cf. *Bursian*, pp. 101 f.

(2) Johannes REUCHLIN, 1455–1522.
   a. Vocabularius breviloquus, synopsis grammaticae Graecae.
   b. Translation of the Batrachomyomachia.
   c. Editions of : *Xenophon*, Apol. Agesil. Hiero ; Aeschinis et Demosthenis oratt. adversariae.

Cf. *L. Geiger*, R., sein Leben u. seine Werke, Berl. 1871; *Bursian*, pp. 120–31.

(3) PHILIP MELANCHTHON, 1497–1560.
   'Praeceptor Germaniae.'
   a. *Institutiones Linguae Graecae*, 1518.   1622[41].
   b. *Grammatica Latina*, 1525.   1757[84].
   c. Editions or commentaries to : Aristoph. Clouds, Plutos ; *Arist.* Ethics and Politics ; Hesiod ; Theognis ; Dem. Olynth. I., in Aristog.; Lycurgos in Leocratem ; Aratus. — *Cic.* de off., de orat., de am., Orator, Topica, Epist. ad fam., orations ; Terence ; Virgil ; Ovid's Fasti ; Sallust ; Quint. Inst. Bk. X ; Tac. Germ.
   d. Latin translations of : Pindar, Euripides ; speeches in Thucydides; some speeches of Demosth.; Aesch. in Ctesiph.
   e. Handbooks on Rhetoric, Dialectics.

Cf. *Camerarius*, de vita Ph. M. ed. by Th. Strobel, Halle 1877, *Schmid*, Encycl. d. Paedag. IV, 653–78, and esp. *K. Hartfelder*, Ph. M., Berlin, 1889.

(4) Joachim Kammermeister (*Camerarius*), 1500–74.
   a. Editions of : Speeches of Demosth., Sophocles with commentary (1534, 1556), Quintilian with comment. (1534), Cicero, 4 vols. fol., 1540, Herodotus, Thucydides, *Plautus* (1552), Theocritos,

Aristotle's Ethics, Theophrastos, historia rei nummariae.

Cf. *Ritschl*, Opusc. II, 99 ff. III, 67 ff. (On his edition of Plautus); *Bursian*, pp. 185-90. Full list of works in *Pökel*, s.v. pp. 39 f.; *C. Halm*, Munich. Acad. II (1873), 241-273.

(5) Johann Albert *Fabricius*, 1668-1736.
  a. *Bibliotheca Graeca*, 14 vols., 1728 (ed. Harles, 1809, 12 vols., index, 1838). A monumental and still indispensable storehouse of information.
  b. Bibliotheca Latina, 1697 (ed. Ernesti, 1773).
  c. Bibliotheca Lat. med. et infim. aetatis, 1746, 6 vols.
  d. Sextus Empiricus, 1718.

Cf. *H. S. Reimarus*, de vita et scriptis F. Hamburg, 1737; *Creuzer*, pp. 201-5; *Bursian*, pp. 360-4; *Pökel*, s. v.

(6) Johann Mathias *Gesner*, 1691-1761.
  Editions of: *Scriptores rei rusticae*, Horace, Quintilian, Pliny the Younger, Claudianus. *Thesaurus Linguae Latinae*, 2 vols. fol., 1749. Transl. of *Lucian*.

Cf. *Bursian*, pp. 387-93; *F. Paulsen*, Gesch. d. gelehrt. Unterrichts in Deutschl., Lpz. 1885, pp. 427-40.

(7) Johann August *Ernesti*, 1707-81.
  Editions of: Xenophon's Memorab., Arist. Clouds, Homer, Callimachus, Polybius, Tacitus, Sueton., *Cicero*, 1739, 1774, 5 vols., with clavis Ciceroniana (Halle, 1832²). Famous teacher and Latin stylist.

Cf. *Bursian*, pp. 400-4; *Allg. deutsche Biogr.* VI, 235-42.

(8) JOH. JACOB REISKE, 1716-74.
  a. Edition of Constantinos Porphyrogennetos, de cerimoniis aulae Byzantinae, 2 vols., 1754.
  b. Editions of: Theocritos, 2 vols., 1766; *Oratt. Graeci*, 12 vols., 1775.
  c. Editions of: *Plutarch*, 12 vols.; *Dionysius Halic.*, 6 vols.; *Maximos Tyrios*, 2 vols.; Dion. Chrysostomos. 2 vols.; Libanios, 4 vols. (all printed after R.'s death).

d. Translation of : Speeches in Thucyd., Speeches of *Dem. and Aesch.*, 5 vols.

e. *Animadversiones ad auctores Graecos*, 5 vols., 1766.

Cf. *Autobiography*, Lpz. 1783, pp. 818; *Bursian*, pp. 407–16.

(9) JOHANN JOACHIM WINCKELMANN, 1717–68.
Founder of the science of Archaeology.
Die Geschichte der Kunst des Alterthums, 1764.

Cf. *K. Justi*, W., sein Leben. seine Werke und seine Zeitgenossen, 3 vols., Lpz., 1872 (pp. xii+525. 398, pp. vi+440); *Bursian*, pp. 426–36.

(10) JOSEPH HILARIUS ECKHEL, 1737–98.
Founder of the science of Numismatics.
Doctrina nummorum veterum, 8 vols., 1798. 1841[4].

Cf. *Bursian*, pp. 496–99.

(11) CHRISTIAN GOTTLOB HEYNE, 1729–1812.
Editions of : Tibullus, 1755 ; Epictetus, 1756 ; *Virgil*, 4 vols., 1775 ; Pindar [Ps.] *Apollodori Bibliotheca*, 2 vols., 1782, 1802[2]; *Iliad*, 8 vols., 1802 ; *Opusc. Academica*, 6 vols., 1785–1812.

Cf. *A. H. L. Heeren*, Chr. G. Heyne, Göttingen, 1813 (XXII, pp. 522); *Bursian*, pp. 476–500.

(B) THE NEW SCHOOL.
FRIEDRICH AUGUST WOLF, 1739 (200 years after Casaubonus) –1824.

a. Prolegomena to HOMER, 1795.

Cp. *R. Volkmann*, Geschichte u. Kritik der W.'s Prolegg., Lpz. 1874.

b. Demosthenis Leptinea (valuable introduction), 1790.

c. Plato's Symposium, Hesiod's Theogony ; Cicero, Tusc. Disp., *Orations* (Post red., in senatu ad Quirites, de domo sua, de haruspicum responsis, pro Marcello — regarded as spurious by W.) Aristoph. *Clouds;* Casaubonus' Suetonius.

d. Encyclopaedie der Philologie ed. Stockmann, Lpz. 1831.

e. Kleine Schriften, 2 vols., 1869, pp. 1200.

 Cf. *W. Körte*, Leben u. Studien F. A. W.'s des Philologen, 2 vols., Essen, 1833 (pp. 363. 314); *Bursian*, pp. 517-48; *M. Pattison*, Essays I, 337-415.

1. *Grammatico-critical School.*

On *Criticism* and *Hermeneutics:*

 Huet, De optimo genere interpretandi, etc., 1691; *F. Schleiermacher*, Works, III 3, pp. 344 ff.; Hermeneutik u. Kritik, Works, 1 pt. VII, 1838 (pp. xviii+390); *G. Hermann*, de officio interpretis, Opusc. V, 405 ff. VII, 97 ff.; *A. Boeckh*, Opusc. I, 100 ff. V, 248 ff. VII, 262 ff., Encyclopaedie, etc., der phil. Wissensch., pp. 79-263; *H. Sauppe*, Epistola Critica; *C. G. Cobet*, Oratio de arte interpretandi, Leyden, 1847 (pp. 163); *G. Bernhardy*, Grundlinien zur Encycl. der Philol., p. 53 ff.; *J. N. Madvig*, Advers. Critica, I (1871), 8-184; *E. Tournier*, Exercices critiques, Paris, 1875 (pp. 175); *H. Steinthal*, Arten u. Formen der Interpretation (Philol. Versamml. Wiesbaden, 1877, pp. 25-35); *C. von Prantl*, Verstehen u. Beurtheilen, Munich Acad., 1877, pp. 37; *F. Bücheler*, Philolog. Kritik, Bonn, 1878: *Fr. Blass*, Hermeneutik u. Kritik (Iwan Müller's Handbuch) **P**, 147-295.

(1) GOTTFRIED HERMANN, 1772-1848.

 a. Editions of: *Aeschylus*, Soph., *Eurip.* (Hecuba, Herc. fur., Suppl., *Bacchae*, Alcestis, *Ion*), Arist. Clouds, *Plautus'* Trinummus, *Aristotle's Poetics*, *Homeric Hymns*, Lexicon of Photios, Bion and Moschus.

 b. Elementa doctrinae metricae, 1816.

 c. Homeric treatises, 1832, 1840. *Opusc.*, 8 vols., 1827-39. vol. VIII, 1876.

 Cf. *O. Jahn*, Biogr. Aufsätze, Lpz. 1849, pp. 91-132; *Bursian*, p. 575 ff., pp. 666-86; *H. Köchly*, G. H. 1874, pp. 330.

(2) Christian August *Lobeck*, 1781-1860.

 a. Sophocles, Aiax, 1809.

 b. AGLAOPHAMUS, 2 vols., 1829.

c. Paralipomena grammaticae Graecae, 2 vols., 1837.

Cf. *Bursian*, p. 572 ff., 711–713.

(3) AUGUST IMMANUEL BEKKER, 1785–1871.

   a. Text Editions of : Plato, Attic Orators, Aristotle, Sextus Empiricus, Thucydides, Theognis, Aristophanes, Photios, Suidas, Scholia to the Iliad, Cassius Dio, Harpocration, Corpus scriptt. Byzantinorum, 24 vols., Homer (with *digamma* in the text), etc., etc.

Cf. *Bursian*, pp. 658–63; *Pökel*, s. v.

(4) KARL LACHMANN, 1793–1851.

   a. Propertius (1816), *Catullus, Prop., Tibull.*, (1829), Terentianus Maurus.

   b. BETRACHTUNGEN ÜBER HOMER'S ILIAS (mit Zusätzen von M. Haupt), 1837, 1841. 'Epoch-making.'

   c. LUCRETIUS, with critical commentary. 'Immortal masterpiece.'

   d. *Lucilius* (ed. Vahlen), *Gaius*, Babrios.

   e. NEW TESTAMENT (*Methodology of scientific textual criticism*).

Cf. *M. Hertz*, K. L., Berlin, 1851 (pp. x+255, xliii) ; *Bursian*, pp. 789–800; *Briefe an M. Haupt*, ed. I. Vahlen, 1893.

(5) *August Meineke*, 1790–1870.

   a. Editor of : *Strabo*, Athenaeus, Callimachus, *Aristophanes, Fragmenta Comicorum* (with HISTORY OF GREEK COMEDY) 5 vols., 1841, Theocritos, Stobaeus, Stephanus Byzantius, Horace (application of the four-line strophe).

   b. *Analecta Alexandrina*, 1843.

Cf. *F. Ranke*, A. M., Ein Lebensbild, Lpz. 1871 ; *Bursian*, pp. 764–9.

(6) Karl *Wilhelm Dindorf*, 1802–83.

   a. Editor of : Aristophanes, *Poetae scenici graeci*, Demosthenes, 9 vols., 1846–51, *Stephanus Byzan-*

tius, Aristides, Themistius, Lucian, Herodotus, Josephus, *Clemens Alexandrinus*, 4 vols., Eusebius, 4 vols.

   b. Scholia to Odyssey, 1856; *scholia to Iliad*, 4 vols., 1877.

   c. Lexicon Aeschyleum, *Lex. Sophocleum*. New edition of *Stephanus' Greek Thesaurus*, Metra Aesch., Soph., Eur., Aristoph.

      Cf. *Biogr. Jahrb.* VI (1883), pp. 112 ff.; *Bursian*, pp. 861-70.

(7) *Karl Lehrs*, 1802-78.

   a. DE ARISTARCHI STUDIIS HOMERICIS, 1833 (1882³, pp. 505).

   b. Horace, 1869. Transl. of *Plato's Phaedrus and Symposion*.

   c. Die Pindarscholien, Lpz. 1873.

      Cf. *E. Kammer*, Biogr. Jahrb. (1879), pp. 15-28; *Bursian*, pp. 718-24.

(8) FRIEDRICH RITSCHL, 1806-76.

   a. PLAUTUS (*Trinummus*, with famous Prolegg.) PARERGA to Plautus and Terence (*Fabulae Varronianae*, etc.), *Opusc.* II, 782 III, 1-300.

   b. On the literary activity of Varro. Opusc. III, pp. 419-592.

   c. Aeschylus, Septem, 1853.

   d. Priscae latinitatis monumenta epigraphica, 1862. Opusc. vol. V.

   e. On Alexandrian library, Stichometry, etc. Opusc. vol. I.

      Cf. *L. Müller*, F. R., Berlin, 1877; *O. Ribbeck*, F. W. R., Ein Beitrag z. Gesch. der Philologie, 2 vols., Lpz. 1881 (pp. vii+348, viii+591); *Bursian*, pp. 812-40.

(9) JOHANN NICOLAUS MADVIG, 1804-1886.

   a. De Asconii Pediani comment. 1826.

   b. CICERO DE FINIBUS, 1839, 1876².

70   OUTLINES OF THE HISTORY

 c. Emendationes *Livianae*, 1860, 1877².
 d. Livy, ed. Madvig and Ussing, 1866, 1879³, 4 vols.
 e. Latin Grammar, 1843¹. *Greek Syntax*, 1847.
 f. Opusc. Acad. 1887². *Adversaria Critica*, 2 vols., 1873.
 g. Die Verfassung u. Verwaltung des röm. Staates.
 Complete list of his works in Wochenschr. f. class. Philol. IV (1887), p. 285. Cf. *Heiberg*, Biogr. Jahrb. IX (1886), 202-21.

(10) AUGUST NAUCK, 1822–1892.
 a. Aristophanis Byzantii fragmenta, 1848.
 b. Euripides, 1854, 1871³; Sophocles, 1867.
 c. TRAGICORUM GRAECORUM FRAGMENTA, 1856. 1889², with *index tragicae dictionis*, 1892. — His masterpiece and the standard work on the subject.
 d. HOMER (Odyssey, 1874, Iliad, 1877).
 e. Porphyrius, 1886², Lexicon Vindobonense, 1867, Iamblichi de vita Pythagorica, 1884.
 Cf. *Th. Zielinski*, A. N., Berlin, 1893, pp. 67 (= Biogr. Jahrb. XVI). Full list of his writings, 125 in number, pp. 59–65.

2. *Historico-antiquarian School.*
 Bibliography:
 Hübner, Encyclopaedie: Greek and Roman Literature, Grammar, Poetics (pp. 140–75), Religion (pp. 175–84), Greek and Roman Antiquities and History (pp. 184–215, 359–88), Geography (pp. 215–85), Chronology (pp. 286–90), Archaeology (pp. 290–342), Metrology and Numismatics (pp. 342–51), Epigraphy (pp. 351–59). Cp. also *Sal. Reinach*, Manuel de philologie classique, vol. II, Appendice, Paris, 1884 (pp. 310).

(1) BARTHOLD GEORG NIEBUHR, 1776–1831.
 a. ROMAN HISTORY, 3 vols., 1811¹.
 b. Lectures on *Roman History*, 3 vols. (Engl. 1843, Germ. 1846).
 c. Lectures on *Ancient History*, 3 vols., 1851.
 d. Edition of *Fronto*, 1816, Fragmm. of Cicero's Speeches.
 e. Kleine Schriften, 2 vols., 1828.

Cf. *S. Winkworth*, The Life and Letters of B. G. N., 3 vols.,
Lond. 1853; *Bursian*, pp. 647–63; *F. Eyssenhardt*, B. G. N.,
Gotha, 1886; *I. Classen*, B. G. N., Gotha, 1876, pp. 181.

(2) AUGUST BOECKH, 1785–1867.
   a. De Graecae tragoediae principibus, 1806.
   b. Edition of PINDAR, 4 vols., 1811–22.
   c. CORPUS INSCRIPTIONUM GRAECARUM, 4 vols.
   d. PUBLIC ECONOMY OF ATHENS, 2 vols., 1817^1, 1886^3.
   e. Philolaos, 1818.
   f. Metrologische Untersuchungen, 1838; Manetho u. die Hundsternperiode, 1845 ; Zur Gesch. der Mondcyclen, 1856 ; *Opuscula*, 7 vols., 1874.
   g. Encyclopaediae u. Methodologie der Philol. ed. Klussmann, 1886^2 (pp. 884).

Cf. *E. von Leutsch*, Philol. Anz. XVI (1886), 224 ff.; *Bursian*, pp. 687–705; Briefwechsel zwischen A. B. und K. O. Müller, 1883, pp. 442.

(3) Friedrich Gottlieb *Welcker*, 1784–1868.
   a. Die Aeschyleische Trilogie Prometheus, 1824.
   b. Theognis, 1826.
   c. Der *Epische Cyclus*, 2 vol., 1849 (1882^2).
   d. DIE GRIECH. TRAGOEDIEN, 3 vols. (pp. 1614), 1841.
   e. Alte Denkmäler, 5 vols., 1849–64.
   f. Griech. Götterlehre, 3 vols., 1863.
   g. Kleine Schriften, 6 vols. (on *Sappho, Prodicus*, etc.).

Cf. *Reinh. Kékulé*, F. G. W.'s Leben, Lpz. 1880 (pp. 591); *Bursian*, pp. 1029–46.

(4) Karl *Ottfried Müller*, 1797–1840.
   a. Die Dorier, 1824; Die Etrusker, 1828 (1878^2).
   b. Archaeologie der Kunst, 1830 (1878^4).
   c. Aeschylus Eumeniden, 1833.
   d. Varro, de lingua Latina, 1833.

e. FESTUS, 1839.
f. HISTORY OF THE LITERATURE OF ANCIENT-GREECE, Lond. 1840, 3 vols. (1876³ in 3 vols., ed. E. Heitz).

Cf. *Bursian*, pp. 1007-9; *K. Hillebrand*, in the French transl. of (*d*), vol. I, xvii-ccclxxx, Paris, 1865; *M. Hertz*, Index lectionum, Breslau, 1884, pp. 13.

(5) FRANZ BOPP, 1791-1867.
Founder of the science of comparative philology.

Cf. *B. Delbrück*, Einl. in das Sprachstudium, Lpz. 1880; *Lefman*, F. B., 1892.

(6) *Gottfried Bernhardy*, 1800-75.
 a. Eratosthenica, 1822; Dionys. Perieg., 1828; Wissensch. Syntax, 1829.
 b. SUIDAS, 2 vols., 1834-58.
 c. GRIECH. LITERATURGESCHICHTE, 2 vols., 1836-45 (1880).
 d. RÖMISCHE LITERATURGESCH., 2 vols., 1830 (1872⁵).

Cf. *R. Volkmann*, G. B., Halle, 1887 (pp. 160); *Bursian*, p. 776.

(7) *Otto Jahn*, 1813-69.
 a. Edition and commentary of PERSIUS, 1843; *Juvenal*, 1851; Cic. *Orator*, 1851; Florus, 1852; *Livii Periochae*, 1853; *Soph. Electra*, 1861¹ (1872²); *Plato, Symposium*, 1864 (1876²); *Ps. Longinus* Περὶ ὕψους, 1867 (1887²).
 b. *Pausaniae descriptio arcis Athen.*, 1860 (1880²).
 c. Numerous treatises on archaeology and literature (e.g., On the subscriptions in Latin MSS. '*Ueber den Aberglauben des bösen Blicks*').

Cf. *Bursian*, pp. 1070-80; *J. Vahlen*, O. J., Wien, 1870, pp. 24.

(8) THEODOR MOMMSEN, 1817—.
 a. *Röm. Münzwesen*, 1850; ROMAN HISTORY, Vols. I-III⁸, V³ (transl. by Dickson); Römische Chro-

nologie, 1859; *Röm. Forschungen*, 2 vols., RÖM. STAATSRECHT, 3 vols. (pp. 708, 1171, 1336), 1888[8].

b. CORPUS INSCRIPTIONUM LATINARUM, Vol. I, III, VIII, IX.

c. *Monumentum Ancyranum*, 1865[1].

d. *Digesta, Solinus, Iordanes, Cassiodorus.*

e. *Zur Lebengesch. des jüngeren Plinius*, Hermes III, pp. 31–139, etc., etc.

For a full list of his works up to 1887, cf. *C. Zangemeister*, Theodor Mommsen als Schriftsteller, Heidelberg, 1887 (*pp. 60*).

INDEX OF NAMES.

	PAGE
Accius, L.	33
Aelius Stilo, L.	33 f.
Agricola, Rud.	63
Alexander Aetolus	10
Ammonius	17
Anonymus mythographus	17
Antigonus Carystius	9
Apollodorus	16 f.
Apollonius Dyscolos	24
Aristarchus	13 ff.
Aristophanes Byzantius	11 ff.
Aristoteles	7 f. 15. 30
Aristoxenus	8
Arruntius Celsus	38
Asconius Pedianus	36
Asper, Aemilius	38
Ateius Philologus	35
Athenaeus	26
Aurispa, Giovanni	50
Bekker, Immanuel	68
Bentley, Richard	61 f.
Bernhardy, Gottfried	72
Bessarion	48
Boccaccio	49
Boeckh, August	71
Bopp, Franz	72
Bruni, Leonardo	49
Burmann, Peter (the Elder)	59
Burmann, Peter (the Younger)	59
Caecilius Calactinus	24
Caesar, Gaius Iulius	32. 34
Caesellius Vindex	32

	PAGE
Callimachus	10
Camerarius, Ioachim	64 f.
du Cange, Chs. du Fresne	55
Canter, Wilhelm	56
Caper, Flavius	38
Casaubonus, Isaac	54 f.
Cassiodorus	39
Censorinus	38
Chalcondylas, Demetrius	48
Charisius	38
Chrysippos	22
Chrysoloras, Manuel	47 f.
Cicero, M. Tullius	34
Cobet, Gabriel	61
Constantinus Porphyrogennetos	42
Crates Mallotes	22 f.
Cruquius, Iac.	56
Demetrius Magnes	23
Dicaearchus	8
Didymus	18 ff.
Dindorf, Wilhelm	68
Diomedes	38
Dionysius, Aelius	26
Dionysius Halicarnassensis	23
Dionysius Thrax	17. 30
Donatus, Aelius	38
Eckhel, Ioseph Hilarius	66
Elmsley, Peter	62
Erasmus, Desiderius	55 f.
Eratosthenes	10 f.
Ernesti, Iohann August	65
Eustathius	44

INDEX OF NAMES.

	PAGE
Fabricius, Ioh. Albert	65
da Feltre, Vittorino	49
Fenestella	36
Ficinus, Marsilius	50
Filelfo, Francisco	50
Gaisford, Thomas	63
Gaza, Theodorus	48
Gellius, Aulus	38
Gesner, Ioh. Mathias	65
Gorgias	6
Graevius	59
Gronovius, Iacob	58
Gronovius, Ioh. Friedrich	58
Grote, George	63
Grotius, Hugo	58
Harpocration	26
Heinsius, Daniel	57
Heinsius, Nicolaus	58
Hemsterhusius, Tiberius	59
Hephaestion	26
Heracleides Ponticus	8
Hermann, Gottfried	67
Hermippos	16
Herodianus	25
Hesychios Alexandrinus	41
Hesychios Illustris	41
Heyne, Christian Gotlob	66
Hieronymus	39
Hofman-Peerlkamp	61
Hyginus, Iulius	35
Iahn, Otto	72
Iowett, Benjamin	63
Isidorus	39
Iuba	25
Iunius, Hadrianus	56
Kyriacus	50

	PAGE
Lachmann, Karl	68
Lambinus, Dionysius	54
Lascaris, Constantinus	48
Leake, William Martin	62
Lehrs, Karl	69
Lipsius, Iustus	56
Lobeck, Christian August	67
Longinus	26
Lycophron	10
Macrobius	39
Madvig, Ioh. Nicolaus	69
Magister, Thomas	45
Markland, Ieremiah	62
Meineke, August	68
Melanchthon, Philipp	64
Mommsen, Theodor	72
Montfaucon, Bernard de	55
Moschopulus, Manuel	45
Müller, Karl Otfried	71
Munro, H. A. J.	63
Muretus, Marcus Antonius	54
Nauck, August	70
Niebuhr, Barthold Georg	70
Nigidius Figulus	31. 35
Nonius Marcellus	38
Pamphilus	25
Pausanias Atticista	26
Peisistratus	6
Petrarca, Francesco	48
Philetas	9
Philon, Herennius	25
Photios	41
Planudes, Maximus	44
Plato	7. 15
Plethon, Georgios Gemisthios	48
Plinius Secundus (the Elder)	36
Poggio Bracciolini	49

INDEX OF NAMES.

	PAGE		PAGE
Politianus, Angelus	51	Stoics	15. 30
Pollux, Iulius	26	Suetonius Tranquillus	37
Porson, Richard	62	Suidas	42 f.
Praxiphanes	8		
Priscianus	39	Taylor, Iohn	62
Probus, M. Valerius	37	Theon	21
Prodicus	7	Theophrastus	8
Protagoras	7. 31	Triklinios, Demetrius	45
Pseudo Longinus	24	Tryphon	20
		Turnebus, Adrianus	54
Quintilianus, Fabius	37	Tzetzes, Iohannes	43
Reiske, Ioh. Iacob	65	Valckenaer, Ludwig Caspar	60
Remmius Palaemon	37	Valla, Laurentius	50
Reuchlin, Iohannes	64	Varro, M. Terentius	31 f. 34
Ritschl, Friedrich	69	Verrius Flaccus, M.	36
Romanus, Iulius	38	Victorinus, Marius	38
Ruhnken, David	60	Victorius, Petrus	51
		Vossius, Ioh. Gerhard	57
Salmasius, Claudius	57		
Salutatus, Colutius	49	Welcker, Friedrich Gottlieb	71
Scaliger, Ioseph	56 f.	Winckelmann, Ioh. Ioachim	66
Scaurus, Q. Terentius	38	Wolf, Friedrich August	66
Servius	38	Wyttenbach, Daniel	60
Spanheim, Ezechiel	59		
Stephanus (Etienne), Henricus	54	Zenodotus	9
Stephanus, Robertus	53		

ADVERTISEMENTS

P. CORNELII TACITI

DIALOGUS DE ORATORIBUS.

Edited with Prolegomena, critical and exegetical commentary, bibliography and indexes, by Dr. ALFRED GUDEMAN, *Professor of Classical Philology, University of Pennsylvania.*

8vo. Cloth. Price, by mail, postpaid, $3.00.

The Prolegomena deal at length with the history of the 'Dialogus Controversy' and furnish positive proofs, both external and internal, of the Tacitean authorship of the treatise. The adnotatio critica accompanying the text is the most complete yet published.

Contents: Prolegomena on the Question of Authorship (pp. XIII–LXIII), Dramatic Structure, Interlocutors and their Parts (pp. LXIV–LXXXVII), Literary Sources (pp. LXXXVIII–CIII), Style and Language (pp. CIV–CXIX), the MSS. (pp. CXX–CXXXVII), Text with critical apparatus (pp. 1–55), critical and exegetical Commentary (pp. 56–382), Bibliography (pp. 383–390), Index locorum (pp. 391–427), and Index nominum et rerum (pp. 428–447).

The Nation, *New York:* So thoroughly well has the work been done, so carefully has the editor studied the questions by which the little tract is beset, and so clearly and independently has he set forth his conclusions, that we are almost ready to believe that a κτῆμα ἐς ἀεί has at last been obtained in the case of one, at least, of the Latin classics. His critical apparatus in its fulness recalls Wecklein's to Aeschylus. . . . The contents of the book are a credit to American scholarship, and its outer dress calls for thanks to the American publishers.

(Department of Special Publication.)

GINN & COMPANY, PUBLISHERS,

BOSTON, NEW YORK, CHICAGO, LONDON.

Represented by EDWARD ARNOLD, 37 Bedford St., Strand, London, Eng., and OTTO HARRASSOWITZ, Leipzig, Germany.

LATIN TEXT-BOOKS.

COLLEGE SERIES OF LATIN AUTHORS.

For a statement of the aim and plan of this series, and a list of volumes in preparation, see the Announcements.

The Satires and Epistles of Horace.

> Edited by Professor JAMES B. GREENOUGH of Harvard University. 12mo. Cloth. xiv + 306 pages. Mailing Price, $1.35; for introduction, $1.25. TEXT EDITION. Paper. Introduction Price, 40 cents.

WHILE this book takes due account of the literature which has grown up about Horace, it is meant to be distinctly a study of the poet himself, and is intended especially for the college classroom. The commentary assumes that the reader is at a somewhat advanced period in his Latin studies. Matters of grammatical detail occupy therefore a very subordinate place, — except so far as Horace's Latinity marks an important stage in the development of the language, or is a conscious deviation for specific purposes from the ordinary literary usages. On the other hand, the effort is made to trace the motive and sequence of thought in each discourse and letter, and thus to emphasize Horace's reflections upon Roman society at one of its great turning-points, and to make clear the poet's system of conduct and life.

The Brutus of Cicero.

> Edited by Professor MARTIN KELLOGG of the University of California. 12mo. Cloth. xxix + 196 pages. Mailing Price, $1.35; for introd., $1.25. TEXT EDITION. Paper. Introduction Price, 40 cents.

IN the *Brutus*, which was composed in 46 B.C. and purports to be a conversation with Atticus and Brutus, Cicero traces the development of oratory among the Romans down to his own time, with critical notices of about two hundred speakers. The long catalogue is relieved of dryness by the dialogue form, the freedom of digression, and by Cicero's fresh and teeming style.

Professor Kellogg has edited the work especially for college reading. The Introduction touches upon points of interest to those to whom Cicero is no stranger, and contains a full conspectus. The notes deal with the subject-matter, historical relations, and diction of the dialogue rather than with the commonplaces of grammar. Parallel passages are freely given, especially from Cicero's other rhetorical works and from Quintilian.

The Annals of Tacitus, Books I.–VI.

> Edited by the late Professor W. F. ALLEN, of the University of Wisconsin. 12mo. Cloth. xlii + 444 pages. Mailing price, $1.65; for introd., $1.50.
> TEXT EDITION. Paper. 240 pages; introduction price, 40 cents.

THE text of this edition is based upon Halm's edition of 1882; but the manuscript reading has been restored in many instances, and the spelling modified in accordance with the results of the most recent studies. In the commentary an effort has been made to show the development of prose Latin since Cicero; but the distinctive aim has been to present a complete and connected view of the reign of Tiberius, and to trace and explain the successive stages in the deterioration of his character, from the wise and humane ruler of his earlier years to the gloomy and suspicious tyrant with whom all are familiar: to that end, the break in the narrative, caused by the loss of parts of the fifth and sixth Books, has been filled by citations from Dio Cassius, Suetonius, and other writers. The important constitutional and administrative changes of this period receive special attention.

Livy, Books I. and II.

> Edited, with Introduction and Notes, by Professor J. B. GREENOUGH, of Harvard University. 12mo. Cloth. xvii + 270 pages. Mailing price, $1.35; for introduction, $1.25.
> TEXT EDITION. Paper. 163 pages. Introduction price, 40 cents.

THE plan of the College Series contemplates at present two volumes of Livy, one containing Books I. and II., the other Books XXI. and XXII. The first volume, which is now ready, has been edited by Professor Greenough in accordance with his well-known views on the teaching of Latin. The fact that Livy is commonly read by freshmen — that is, by students who are still engaged in learning to read Latin — has been kept steadily in view. Historical questions have been treated with sufficient fulness for intelligent reading; but the discussion of them has been made subordinate to the presentation of Livy's exact ideas in the form in which they lay in his mind, and in the precise order in which in their parts and their totality he intended to present them. The character of early Roman history and Livy's quality as a historian, together with his style and Latinity, are treated in the Introduction.

Livy, Books XXI. and XXII.

Edited, with Introduction and Notes, by Professor J. B. GREENOUGH, of Harvard University, and Professor TRACY PECK, of Yale University. 12mo. Cloth. xiv + 232 pages. Mailing price, $1.35; for introduction, $1.25.

TEXT EDITION. Paper. 232 pages. Introduction price, 40 cents.

THE scope and method of this book have been illustrated in the volume of Livy already published. The immediate needs of the learner are recognized throughout, — that he may appreciate the power and charm of Livy's narrative, and acquire the art of reading Latin *as* Latin. He is helped also to enter with intelligent sympathy into the workings of Livy's mind, and his conception of his country's history and destiny. Due attention is also given to the great duel between Rome and Carthage that gives to these books of Livy an exceptional historical value.

The text is based upon the recension by August Luchs of the Codex Puteanus and of its best derivatives.

Catullus.

Edited, with Introduction and Notes, by Professor ELMER T. MERRILL, of Wesleyan University. 12mo. Cloth. 1 + 273 pages. Mailing price, $1.50; for introduction, $1.40.

TEXT EDITION. Paper. 273 pages. Introduction price, 40 cents.

THE text of this edition has been prepared with particular care, mainly on the authority of the two best codices, G and O, the latter having been collated by the editor himself at Oxford in the summer of 1889 by the courtesy of the Librarian of the Bodleian. The work is furnished with an introduction, in which the poet's life and character, his relations with his contemporaries, his literary activity, and the manuscript traditions of his poems are fully treated, and an exposition of his metres is given. The Appendix contains a complete collation of G and O, and a reduced *fac-simile* of a page of the latter codex, reduced one-third in size, forms the frontispiece of the volume. There are two indexes, one of the proper names mentioned in the introduction or in the text; the other, of the matters treated in the notes.

COLLEGE SERIES OF GREEK AUTHORS.

EDITED BY

Professor JOHN WILLIAMS WHITE AND

Professor THOMAS D. SEYMOUR.

THIS series will include the works either entire or selected of all the Greek authors suitable to be read in American colleges. The volumes contain uniformly an Introduction, Text, Notes, Rhythmical Schemes where necessary, an Appendix including a brief bibliography and critical notes, and a full Index. In accordance with the prevailing desire of teachers, the notes are placed below the text, but to accommodate all, and, in particular, to provide for examinations, the text is printed and bound separately, and sold at the nominal price of forty cents. In form the volumes are a square octavo. All except text editions are bound both in cloth and in paper. Large Porson type, and clear diacritical marks emphasize distinctions and minimize the strain upon the student's eyes. As the names of the editors are a sufficient guaranty of their work, and as the volumes thus far issued have been received with uniform favor, the Publishers have thought it unnecessary to publish recommendations. *Texts are supplied free to professors for classes using the text and note editions.* See also the Announcements.

The Clouds of Aristophanes.

Edited on the basis of Kock's edition. By M. W. HUMPHREYS, Professor in University of Virginia. Square 8vo. 252 pages. Cloth: Mailing Price, $1.50; Introduction, $1.40. Paper, $1.20 and $1.10. **Text Edition**: 88 pages. Paper: Mailing Price, 45 cents; Introduction, 40 cents.

SINCE the place of Aristophanes in American Colleges is not definitely fixed, the Commentary is adapted to a tolerably wide range of preparation.

The Bacchantes of Euripides.

Edited on the basis of Wecklein's edition. By I. T. BECKWITH, Professor in Trinity College. Square 8vo. 146 pages. Cloth: Mailing Price, $1.35; Introduction, $1.25. Paper, $1.00 and 95 cents. **Text Edition**: 64 pages. Paper: Mailing Price. 45 cents; Introduction, 40 cents.

THE Introduction and Notes aim, first of all, to help the student understand the purport of the drama as a whole, and the place each part occupies in the development of the poet's plan; and in the second place, while explaining the difficulties, to encourage in the learner a habit of broader study.

Introduction to the Language and Verse of Homer.

By THOMAS D. SEYMOUR, Hillhouse Professor of Greek in Yale College. Square 8vo. 104 pages. Cloth: Mailing Price, 80 cents; Introduction, 75 cents. Paper: 65 cents and 60 cents.

THIS is a practical book of reference designed primarily to accompany the forthcoming edition of Homer in the College Series of Greek Authors, but equally well adapted to any other edition. It clears away many of the student's difficulties by explaining dialectic forms, metrical peculiarities, and difficult points in Homeric style and syntax, with carefully chosen examples.

The Table of Contents occupies one page; the Index ten pages.

Homer's Iliad, Books I.–III. and Books IV.–VI.

Both edited on the basis of the Ameis-Hentze edition, by THOMAS D SEYMOUR, Hillhouse Professor of Greek in Yale College. Square 8vo. Books I.–III. 235 pages. Cloth: Mailing price, $1.50; for introduction, $1.40. Paper: $1.20 and $1.10.
Books IV.–VI. 214 pages. Cloth: Mailing price, $1.50; for introduction, $1.40. Paper: $1.20 and $1.10.
Text Edition of each. 66 pages. Paper: Mailing price, 45 cents; for introduction, 40 cents.

THE editor has made many additions to the German edition in order to adapt the work more perfectly to the use of American classes. But he has endeavored to aid the teacher in doing scholarly work with his classes, not to usurp the teacher's functions. References have been made to the editor's Homeric Language and Verse for the explanation of Epic forms. Illustrations have been drawn freely from the Old Testament, from Vergil, and from Milton. A critical Appendix and an Index are added.

The second of these volumes contains the only full commentary published in this country on Books IV.–VI.

Homer's Odyssey, Books I.–IV.

Edited on the basis of the Ameis-Hentze edition. By B. PERRIN, Professor of Greek in Yale College. Square 8vo. 230 pages. Cloth: Mailing Price, $1.50; Introduction, $1.40. Paper: $1.20 and $1.10. **Text Edition**: 75 pages. Paper: Mailing Price, 45 cents; Introduction, 40 cents.

THE German edition has been freely changed to adapt it to the needs of American college classes, but record is made in the appendix of all important deviations from the opinions of the German editors. References are rather liberally given to the leading American grammars, and also to Monro's *Homeric Grammar*. As the gist of matter referred to is always given in the current note, such references are usually meant for those who desire to collect further illustrative material. Much attention has been paid to the indication or citation of **iterati**, conventional phrases, and metrical **formulæ**. The student should realize in some measure both the bulk of this material, and its bearing on the critical analysis of the poem. The latest accepted views in Homeric Archæology are presented. The Appendix gives not only strictly critical data, but also material which should enable a student with limited apparatus to understand the historical and literary status of controverted views.

The Apology and Crito of Plato.

Edited on the basis of Cron's edition. By LOUIS DYER, Formerly Assistant-Professor in Harvard University. Square 8vo. iv + 204 pages. Cloth: Mailing Price, $1.50; Introduction, $1.40. Paper: $1.20 and $1.10. **Text Edition**: 50 pages. Paper: Mailing Price, 45 cents; Introduction, 40 cents.

THIS edition gives a sketch of the history of Greek philosophy before Socrates, a Life of Plato and of Socrates, a summarized account of Plato's works, and a presentation of the Athenian law bearing upon the trial of Socrates. Its claims to the attention of teachers rest, first, upon the importance of Schanz's latest critical work, which is here for the first time made accessible — so far as the *Apology* and *Crito* are concerned — to English readers, and second, upon the fulness of its citations from Plato's other works, and from contemporary Greek prose and poetry. For learners it provides the stimulus of constant illustration from familiar English literature, and the more indispensable discipline derived from a full explanation of grammatical and idiomatic difficulties.

The Protagoras of Plato.

Edited on the basis of Sauppe's edition, with additions. By Professor J. A. TOWLE, Teacher of Greek in Westminster School, Dobb's Ferry, N.Y. Square 8vo. 175 pages. Cloth: Mailing price, $1.35; for introduction, $1.25. Paper: $1.05 and 95 cents.
Text Edition: 69 pages. Paper: By mail, 45 cents; for introd., 40 cents.

THE *Protagoras* is perhaps the liveliest of the dialogues of Plato. In few dialogues is the dramatic form so skilfully maintained without being overborne by the philosophical development. By the changing scenes, the variety in the treatment of the theme, and the repeated participation of the bystanders, the representation of a scene from real life is vivaciously sustained.

Noticeable, too, is the number of vividly elaborated characters: Socrates, ever genial, ready for a contest, and toying with his opponents. Protagoras, disdainful toward the other sophists, condescending toward Socrates. Prodicus, surcharged with synonymic wisdom. Hippias, pretentious and imposing. The impetuous Alcibiades and the tranquil Critias.

Herr Geheim-Rath Sauppe is the Nestor of German philologists, and his Introduction and Commentary have been accepted as models by scholars.

The Antigone of Sophocles.

Edited on the basis of Wolff's edition. By MARTIN L. D'OOGE, Ph.D., Professor of Greek in the University of Michigan. Square 8vo. 196 pages. Cloth: Mailing price, $1.50; for introduction, $1.40. Paper: $1.20 and $1.10. **Text Edition**: 59 pages. Paper: Mailing price, 45 cents; for introduction, 40 cents.

THE Commentary has been adapted to the needs of that large number of students who begin their study of Greek tragedy with this play. The Appendix furnishes sufficient material for an intelligent appreciation of the most important problems in the textual criticism of the play. The rejected readings of Wolff are placed just under the text. The rhythmical schemes are based upon those of J. H. Heinrich Schmidt.

Thucydides, Book I.

Edited on the basis of Classen's edition. By the late CHARLES D. MORRIS, M.A. (Oxon.), Professor in the Johns Hopkins University. Square 8vo. 353 pages. Cloth: Mailing price, $1.75; for introduction, $1.65. Paper: $1.45 and $1.35. **Text Edition**: 91 pages. Paper: Mailing price, 45 cents; for introduction, 40 cents.

Thucydides, Book III.

Edited on the basis of Classen's edition. By CHARLES FORSTER SMITH, Ph.D., Professor of Greek, University of Wisconsin. Square 8vo. 320 pages. Cloth: Mailing price, $1.75; for introduction, $1.65. **Text Edition**: 75 pages. Paper: Mailing price, 45 cents; for introduction, 40 cents.

Thucydides, Book V.

Edited on the basis of Classen's edition. By HAROLD NORTH FOWLER, Ph.D., Professor of Greek, Western Reserve University. Square 8vo. 213 pages. Cloth: Mailing price, $1.50; for introduction, $1.40. Paper: $1.20 and $1.10. **Text Edition**: 67 pages. Paper: Mailing price, 45 cents; for introduction, 40 cents.

Thucydides, Book VII.

Edited on the basis of Classen's edition. By CHARLES FORSTER SMITH, Ph.D., Professor of Greek, University of Wisconsin. Square 8vo. 202 pages. Cloth: Mailing price, $1.50; for introduction, $1.40. Paper: $1.20 and $1.10. **Text Edition**: 68 pages. Paper: Mailing price, 45 cents; for introduction, 40 cents.

THE main object of these editions of Books I., III., V., and VII. of Thucydides is to render Classen's Commentary accessible to English-speaking students. His text has been followed with few exceptions. The greater part of his notes, both exegetical and critical, are translated in full. But all the best commentaries on Thucydides, and the literature of the subject generally have been carefully studied to secure the best and latest results of Thucydidean research. Frequent reference is made not only to the standard grammars published in the United States, but also to the larger works of Krüger and Kühner.

Xenophon, Hellenica, Books I.-IV.

Edited on the basis of the edition of Büchsenschütz, by J. IRVING MANATT, Ph.D., LL.D., Professor of Greek Literature and History in Brown University. Square 8vo. 300 pages. Cloth: Mailing price, $1.75; for introduction, $1.65. Paper: $1.45 and $1.35. **Text Edition**: 138 pages. Paper: Mailing price, 45 cents; for introduction, 40 cents.

THIS work, treating of an extremely interesting period of Greek history, is admirably adapted to classes in rapid reading. The Commentary deals largely with the history and antiquities of the period, but provides grammatical information and suggestion for the review and inculcation of grammatical principles. Very full indexes are added.

Xenophon, Hellenica, Books V.-VII.

Edited on the basis of the edition of Büchsenschütz by CHARLES E. BENNETT, Professor of Latin in Cornell University. Square 8vo. 240 pages. Cloth: Mailing price, $1.50; for introduction, $1.40. Paper: $1.20 and $1.10.
Text Edition. 128 pages. Paper. Mailing price, 45 cents; for introduction, 40 cents.

IMPORTANT additions have been made in this edition to the notes of Büchsenschütz in the way of material drawn from other sources, particularly from the commentaries of Breitenbach, Kurz, and Grosser. Special attention has been paid to the language. The orthography has been made to correspond as closely as possible with the Attic usage of Xenophon's day, as determined by the testimony of contemporary inscriptions, while syntactical peculiarities receive careful consideration. An Introduction by the American editor gives a review of the salient events in the history of the important period covered by the text. Besides an Appendix devoted to matters of textual criticism, the book contains a full grammatical index and an index of proper names.

The Prometheus Bound of Æschylus.

With the Fragments of the *Prometheus Loosed*. With Introduction and Notes by N. WECKLEIN, Rector of the Maximilian Gymnasium in Munich. Translated by F. D. ALLEN, Professor of Classical Philology in Harvard University. Square 8vo. iv + 179 pages. Cloth. Mailing price, $1.50; for introduction, $1.40. Paper, $1.20 and $1.10.
Text Edition. i + 57 pages. Paper. Mailing price, 45 cents; for introduction, 40 cents.

THE book is a translation, with some freedom as to form of expression, of Wecklein's second edition (1878). A few changes in text and commentary have been requested by the German editor, and references to American grammatical works, replacing in some cases the original references to Krüger, have been added by the translator. In the transcription of the metrical schemes into the notation commonly used in this country, the translator has assumed a somewhat greater responsibility than elsewhere, but here too he has endeavored to follow the editor's intentions. The copious explanatory commentary is followed by a critical appendix.